John Sandfield Macdonald

BRUCE W. HODGINS

John Sandfield Macdonald

1812-1872

Canadian Biographical Studies
University of Toronto Press

Printed in Canada

ISBN 0-8020-3248-6

CANADIAN BIOGRAPHICAL STUDIES

Edited by Alan Wilson and André Vachon

John Strachan 1778–1867, J. L. H. HENDERSON
Michel Barrin de la Galissonière 1693–1756, LIONEL GROULX
John Sandfield Macdonald 1812–1872, BRUCE W. HODGINS
Henry Alline 1748–1784, J. M. BUMSTED

Foreword

The *Canadian Biographical Studies* is allied with the project of the *Dictionary of Canadian Biography/Dictionnaire biographique du Canada.*

These small volumes are designed primarily to interest the general reader, and they will be published in two languages. They seek to fill a gap in our knowledge of men who seemed often to be merely secondary figures, frequently non-political contributors to our regional and national experience in Canada. Our social, educational, and economic history may perhaps be better understood in their light.

In these *Studies*, the emphasis is upon an interpretation rather than a life. The limitation in size challenges the author to consider the best use of anecdote, description of place, reference to general history, and use of quotation. The general reader will be offered the fruits of recent research. Not all of the volumes will aim at full comprehensiveness and completeness: some may be followed later by larger and fuller studies of the subject. Many of the present studies, it is hoped, may suggest new interpretive possibilities not only about the central figure but also about his period.

The editors have not followed two of Plutarch's chief standards: the subjects of these *Studies* have not been chosen only for their public virtue, or for their acknowledged distinction. Most of them lived out their lives in Canada, but the careers of some were conducted partly in other theatres. Some have been chosen because, though they were once widely known, they have since been undeservedly neglected.

Some have been selected not for their obvious leadership or eminence, but because they were sufficiently prominent to represent qualities that guided their age: men of significance if not of first prominence. Some have been grouped in studies that should throw light on interesting families, professional groups, or lobbies in our past.

Thus, the *Studies* is not a series of biography alone, but of social, economic and political history approached through the careers and ideas – acknowledged, but often unrecognized – of Canadians of many ranks and diverse times.

ALAN WILSON

Contents

	FOREWORD	v
	ACKNOWLEDGMENTS	ix
I	The Member from Glengarry	3
II	Responsible Government with Irresponsible Ministers	23
III	The Baldwinites and the Mauves	40
IV	The Premier from Cornwall	56
V	On the Sidelines	75
VI	'What the Hell has Strathroy Done for Me?'	89
VII	'Upright and Zealous'	119
	A BIBLIOGRAPHICAL NOTE	125
	INDEX	127

Acknowledgments

I am indebted to many people and institutions for their assistance in helping me to produce this study. Only a few can be mentioned. My doctoral dissertation carried the story of John Sandfield Macdonald's political career, in much more detail than is possible here, to the fall of his government in March 1864; I was particularly indebted in its preparation to Professor W. B. Hamilton, Duke University's Commonwealth Studies Center, and the Canada Council. For ten years Mrs Babette Brodie of the 'Drumming Partridge,' Combermere, who as one of Sandfield Macdonald's great-granddaughters has had a deep and candid interest in her family's and country's past, has been a source of assistance and inspiration to me. Mrs Helen Small, now in Dar es Salaam, who first began the serious study of Sandfield Macdonald and has produced a brilliant thesis on the Confederation elections in Ontario, helped me over several troublesome spots. Professor Elwood Jones, now my colleague, has frequently over the years assisted me from his vast knowledge of biographical details of provincial Canada and his general archival lore. Mrs Sandra Gillis, my research assistant and former student, showed diligence, independence, resourcefulness and commitment far beyond what I had a right to expect. Mrs Eileen Allemang cheerfully and with great interest typed most of the manuscript several times. Miss Melody Morrison, also a former student, helped me with the index. The staff of the public archives of both Canada and Ontario were always helpful. Trent University assisted me in many ways. Finally, Carol, my wife, was a constant source of encouragement.

Peterborough, November 1969 B. W. H.

John Sandfield Macdonald

1

The Member from Glengarry

In July 1867 John Sandfield Macdonald became the first premier of the new Province of Ontario. To many he seemed a strange choice, even though he had had vast legislative experience. He had been elected initially in 1841 to the first legislature of the Province of Canada, following the Act of Union. That British statute had joined Upper and Lower Canada into an organic, single if culturally artificial entity. Sandfield was the only member who served in the united province's eight stormy parliaments. Now that province, torn asunder by centrifugal forces and political paralysis, had passed into history, replaced by the dominion of Canada with its four provinces, two Maritime and two old Canadian. Although John Sandfield was a Reformer, and the majority of Upper Canadian or Ontario votes tended to favour Reformers, he was not the Reform leader. Ontario Reform really had no single leader, but George Brown, the fiery editor of the Toronto *Globe*, led the largest group, those who called themselves Grits. In 1867, there existed between Brown and Sandfield a long lasting and deep enmity. Most of the Grits opposed Sandfield's coalition government. In fact, Sandfield largely owed his office to the efforts of his namesake, now Prime Minister Sir John A. Macdonald. Yet this Conservative chieftain had long opposed Sandfield across the narrow aisle of the old Canadian assembly. Furthermore, Sandfield had resisted Confederation, arguing that federalism was costly and wasteful, that it was being instituted without popular endorsation, and that it would split the economic unity of 'Central Canada,' the valleys of the St Lawrence and Ottawa centred on Montreal. Now he was premier of Confederation's strongest province, one whose inhabitants had often shown a decided tendency toward localism or what was to become known as provincial rights. The first premier of Ontario was a Roman Catholic, admittedly a liberal or only nominal Catholic who was personally disinclined toward separate schools, but still a Catholic. Old Upper Canada, both Grit Reform and Orange Conservative, was militantly Protestant. The great cry of many Upper Canadians for fifteen years had been representation by population, but Sandfield had long resisted it for a bicultural country; he claimed that alone it was unworkable because it would require too much trust by the French-speaking minority of the English-speaking majority.

Even from the point of view of geography, Sandfield seemed to be a strange choice as premier; he represented Cornwall, the province's easternmost town, and like other men of substance in that area, he looked down river to Montreal for his metropolis, not upward to Toronto, the Queen City of the west. Ontario was looking westward to the future, but its premier seemed to have his greatness behind him. The peak of his career had come with his service as premier of the province of Canada, from 1862 to 1864. His resignation in March 1864 had set off the chain reaction leading to the political reorganization of British North America.

The incongruity of his premiership matched, in a sense, his personal appearance. Towering six foot three with legs peculiarly thin, or cadaverous as a critic said, for sustaining such a trunk, he always wore in public the high 'neck-choker' collar that long before Confederation had become old-fashioned. His gaunt features, large grey side whiskers, and silvering dark brown hair adorned a face which the same unkind critic described as 'containing an area something less than an acre.' In keeping with his 'attenuated' legs, he had fingers inordinately long and talon-like.[1] For about a decade now he had had the use of only one lung, and this serious infirmity caused him to walk with a shuffling gait, one shoulder held considerably higher than the other. He was not healthy. Yet, looking carefully and compassionately at the wiry premier, a man who was old at 54, one could see in the flashing dark grey eyes, the pleasing countenance, and the heavy locks of hair, something of the tall, comely royal messenger of nearly

1 *London Advertiser*, 13 Feb. 1869.

thirty years past. Sandfield at that time had won the heart of a genteel and most desirable Southern belle, who for him defied a proud Louisiana father and eloped with the young Scot from Canada, climbing over the garden wall of her school in Baltimore.

Unlike most of his English-speaking political contemporaries, John Sandfield Macdonald was Canadian-born. From his youth he was fully committed to Canada, to a monarchical Canada linked to the British crown. Not of Loyalist stock, this Canadian of Highland Scottish parentage did not generally relate political matters to the narrow question of loyalty. If his vision of a transcontinental nation was faulty or reserved for some more auspicious future, he had before 1866 the firm conviction that the province of Canada could survive as a unitary state. It could preserve the economic unity of the non-American part of the St Lawrence valley if only its people would show toleration, eschew dogmatism, especially religious and cultural dogmatism, and accept the benefits of a plural society. In this plural society, the French, who dominated the old Lower Canadian portion of the province numerically, had a permanent place, and this French fact required clear political recognition. To survive and prosper, Canada could never be a country of the melting pot, run by the simple numerical majority. Broad, honest, principled parties, using the legitimate tool of Victorian patronage, should unite men of different cultures, religions, and regions rather than separate them. Although caustic, irascible, and thin-skinned in his personal relations, at times coarse and uncouth in his language, although driven at times to refer to himself as a political Ishmaelite, Sandfield was one of the few Upper Canadian Reformers able to hold the political friendship of English and French Canadians of various backgrounds and persuasions.

John Sandfield Macdonald was born in St Raphael's West on 12 December 1812. Part of the explanation of his career lies amid the stony hills around unpretentious St Raphael's. Situated in Charlottenburg, one of the two townships of the county of Glengarry fronting on the St Lawrence, St Raphael's was once the centre of Roman Catholicism in Upper Canada. The village lies eight miles north of the widening of the river called Lake St Francis, and about the same distance from the boundary of Quebec. To the south the land falls away in a gentle slope. A tiny stream trickles through a north-south valley on either side of which are the few buildings of the settlement. Although knolls and ridges to the south eliminate most of the distant view, one can see against the sky, here and there on the sides of the valley, the blue and purple peaks of the Precambrian Adirondacks of New York State, far beyond the lake. To the north the land quickly becomes stony and rough, with limestone outcroppings. Only with great difficulty do most of the hardy folk of the back townships of Glengarry wrest a living from the reluctant soil. St Raphael's tall and impressive Georgian-colonial church, built of limestone and completed around 1821, long stood on the western edge of the valley as a reminder of earlier importance.

When Sandfield was born Upper Canadians were at war. They were fighting against their cousins, some of whom lived among the purple hills across the lake. Two months before his birth, the battle of Queenston Heights had claimed the life of a famous Glengarrian, Colonel John Macdonell (Greenfield), acting attorney general and aide-de-camp of General Brock, who was also killed. Because in Glengarry the loyal military tradition ran inordinately deep, inhabitants of the county played a more significant role in the war than did the militiamen from most other areas. It was not strange, therefore, that Sandfield received his first name in honour of the fallen chieftain.

Glengarry had been settled by about 1,500 Scottish Loyalists, refugees from the American republic. Both Presbyterian and Roman Catholic Loyalists had fled to the area, but the most important group had been the various Catholic families of the Clan Macdonell of Glengarry living in the Mohawk valley after the days of Highland deprivation following 'the Forty-five.' Reconciled in America to the House of Hanover, and to George III in particular, they had formed the backbone of the King's Royal Regiment of New York and of the Royal Highland Regiment. They had carried with them to the old Province of Quebec their military discipline and hierarchical social organization. Spacious and elegant houses, built by the chieftains or colonels of the militia, began to appear along the front, giving it a certain rustic, frontier splendour. In 1786 other Highlanders began to arrive direct from Scotland; these included the 500 parishioners of the poverty-ridden village of Knoydart with their priest and leader, Father Alexander Macdonell (Scotus). The centre of this post-Loyalist settlement was naturally farther inland, and the priest of Knoydart became the priest of St Raphael's West, with a parish stretching far to the west.

Allan Macdonald of Clan Ranald, not Clan Glengarry like the Loyalists, and his son Alexander Sandfield were among those from Knoydart who settled at St Raphael's. (Likely of old country origin, the name Sandfield became a sub-surname like those of the more established Macdonells, such as Scotus, Leek, Abercalder and Greenfield.) Young Alexander married Nancy Macdonald, daughter of another villager and distant cousin, called John Macdonald. A small farmer, Alexander owned lot seven, west of the church's lot six, both of which lay near the top of the western slope of the valley on the edge of the village itself. The King's Road, which cut through both lots, separated the Sandfield homestead to the north from the church to the south. It was here that Nancy delivered her first born, John Sandfield. Here also were born four other children of the marriage, Ranald Sandfield, Donald Alexander, Alexander Francis, and a girl who died.

In 1820 the frail, spritely and devout Nancy Macdonald herself died, the apparent victim of a chilling winter sleigh ride. Left without a mother at eight years of age, young John grew up noted for his independent, undisciplined spirit. At eleven he attempted to run away from his heavy-handed father and was carried back forcibly. Soon afterwards he was caught negotiating with an Indian at Cornwall to paddle him to the American side; the Indian wanted 50 cents, but John had only 25. He attended the parish school for a few years, and at the age of sixteen obtained a job in Lancaster, a few miles to the southeast, as a clerk in a general store and post office. He then moved to a similar position in Cornwall. Here he was apparently humiliated by the jibes of the street children who called him a 'counter hopper' and pelted him with snowballs. Urged on by a lawyer who frequented the store, John Sandfield decided to prepare himself for the study of law. He enrolled in November 1832 as a special student in the Eastern District Grammar School at Cornwall.

Sandfield was now almost twenty years old. The war had been over for eighteen years, and the front townships of the counties of Stormont, Dundas and Glengarry, which together made up the provincial sub-division known as the Eastern District, had passed out of the pioneer era. The brief moment of glory had already ended for St

Raphael's West. Its third priest, another Alexander Macdonell, a dynamic and tolerant man who had become famous as a militia chaplain during the war and had built St Raphael's great stone church, had been made the first bishop of Upper Canada. But in 1829 the episcopal seat was transferred to Kingston. Cornwall, with a population of about 1,000 and situated in Stormont but near the Glengarry line, developed unchallenged as the main town of the district. A principal trans-shipping spot for the interior, it was one day's journey west of Montreal, whether one travelled smoothly in winter by sleigh or in summer part way by rough stage from the city to Coteau du Lac and then by steamboat. West from Cornwall, one generally took the stage to Prescott, by-passing the entire International Rapids. But in the thirties small steamers began running that part of the turbulent river lying between Dickinson's Landing and Prescott. Between Cornwall and Dickinson's Landing, a distance of twelve miles, lay the majestic and unascendable Long Sault.

The secondary school Sandfield was now attending in Cornwall was well known. First established in 1803 by John Strachan, it had become in 1807 the public institution for the district. After a period of decline, it was restored to prominence and high academic standing by the Rev. Hugh Urquhart, a Church of Scotland minister who became principal in 1821 and remained until 1840. Many of the future leaders of the Family Compact studied in the Cornwall Grammar School. Dr Urquhart allowed John Sandfield, who had insufficient financial resources and whom he regarded as 'a deserving and favourite pupil,'[2] to postpone payment of most of his tuition fees until 1838, four years after his graduation at the top of his class.

Accepted as a student-at-law by the Law Society of Upper Canada, Dr Urquhart's prize pupil was articled in the fall of 1835 to Archibald McLean, veteran of Queenston Heights, leading tory lawyer of Cornwall and legislative assemblyman. In April 1837, however, after a term as speaker, McLean secured appointment to the Court of King's Bench. The new judge used his considerable influence with government to secure for the young man a commission to act as a queen's messenger carrying dispatch cases between the lieutenant governor

2 Public Archives of Canada (henceforth PAC),
John Sandfield Macdonald–Langlois Papers (henceforth JSM Papers),
Urquhart to JSM, 25 Oct. 1838.

in Toronto and the British minister in Washington. In September 1837, after this American trip, Sandfield wistfully but excitedly visited St Raphael's to take leave of his boyhood home 'perhaps forever.' He was now to serve as McLean's assistant on the judge's first western circuit, and this experience was to be of considerable importance to him later.

Fortunately, a diary of his journey survives, giving a vivid description of his impressions.[3] He travelled by stage along the river portage route and over the bumpy roads of the Western Peninsula, by American portage railroad along the Niagara frontier, and by crowded and luxurious lake steamers. He saw the rising American communities on the Lake Erie and Detroit shores 'to which the Yankees give the name of Towns and Cities,' and he disapproved of the speculation and the wild abandon in the region; he feared that ruin would now result from the crash of early 1837. Nevertheless, he contrasted American expansion with the apparent lethargy and the few scattered houses 'on our side of the River.' In Sandwich, London, and Hamilton he enjoyed the business of the courts, flirted with the young ladies, and met many of the provincial personalities in social events connected with the circuit, including Speaker Allan MacNab, who was acting as crown prosecutor, and Colonel Thomas Talbot, the baron of Lake Erie. On board ship returning to Toronto, Sandfield won nineteen dollars in a long card game with the judge, Solicitor General 'Sweet William' Henry Draper and the great entrepreneur Isaac Buchanan. Only the 'approach of the Sabbath warned us to quit,' he wrote.

On the trip he was apparently unaware that rebellion was about to erupt in parts of the Canadas. When it came in December, it was decisively crushed, but for much of the next year the border with the United States was tense. In January 1838 Sandfield was commissioned as a lieutenant in the Queen's Light Infantry, a Toronto militia unit. About the same time and through the efforts again of Archibald McLean, Sandfield began his articling with W. H. Draper.

He also acted several more times as queen's messenger, carrying dispatches to New York and Washington. On one occasion, under armed escort, a stop was made at the fashionable Saratoga Springs.

3 JSM Papers. A version edited by George W. Spragge appeared as 'A Diary of 1837 by John Sandfield Macdonald' in *Ontario History*, XLVII (March 1955), 1–11.

Here the 25-year-old Canadian met 18-year-old Marie Christine Waggaman. She was vacationing with her father, George Augustus Waggaman from Louisiana, and her two sisters. The dark and lanky messenger and the gay and charming young lady were soon madly in love.[4] The stern but solicitous Waggaman was not impressed. He was deeply attached to Christine, and he had other plans for her. While attending Mlle Bujac's French finishing school in Baltimore, where she was a focus of attention and to which she was now returned, she had been betrothed to Teakle Wallis, an eligible Baltimore lawyer. The school was a logical place for Christine. Her father was of old and respected Maryland stock. He had served with Andrew Jackson in the battle of New Orleans and had then settled in Louisiana. A lawyer, a state judge, a state secretary, from 1832 to 1835 a United States senator, and a Whig who was a friend of Daniel Webster, Waggaman was a grower of sugar cane. Christine's mother, the former Camille Armault, was linked prominently to old French Louisiana, and her maternal grandmother, Christina, was the daughter of the Baron de Brounner, one-time commander of Spanish forces in Louisiana and of Maria Carbonara de Spinola of Genoa. On the Waggamans' 'Avondale' plantation, Christine's first language had been French, and it was to remain her primary tongue. Whether at Avondale or in Baltimore, life for Christine was French, Catholic, and genteel. For the moment the thwarted Sandfield could do nothing about his American love. There was some danger of war between Britain and the United States. Several of the irregular American incursions into the provinces were bloody. Early in 1839, following the repulsion of a raid at Windsor, Sandfield, in fact, spent some time 'doing the soldier on that frontier.'[5]

In the spring of 1840, having completed with distinction his articling with Draper, he established a law office in Cornwall. It was a propitious time, because the town was abustle with the construction of the Cornwall Canal along the waterfront and upstream past the Long Sault; it was brought into use in 1842, though most steamers shot the rapids going downstream. In June 1840 he was called to the provin-

4 PAC, Notes of Cecily Langlois (widow of Eugene Langlois, JSM's grandson), 'The Romance of John Sandfield Macdonald and an outline of his wife's Antecedents as told me by his daughter Josephine.'

5 PAC, John A. Macdonald Papers (henceforth Macdonald Papers), JSM to Sir John A. Macdonald (henceforth Macdonald), 6 Nov. 1871.

cial bar. He was also appointed first lieutenant of the newly-formed local volunteer fire brigade. But one fire, the fire of love, Sandfield was not planning to extinguish. He had seen Christine whenever he could act as royal messenger. Passing through Baltimore he would pose as a relative and thereby obtain time with her. In the fall of 1840 they eloped and were married in New York. A year after Christine's marriage Teakle Wallis wrote her a complimentary letter, referring to her 'old triumphs' and praising her beauty, charm, and lively conversation; Sandfield he described as 'the very happy man, your high lord.'[6] Proud Waggaman, who was in economic difficulties on the plantation, was deeply offended by his daughter's disobedience. Her mother, although saddened by the physical separation, quickly adjusted to the happy match, but reconciliation with her father was never complete. In March 1843 a leading Louisiana Democrat killed Waggaman, the Whig, on the duelling grounds of New Orleans. Mrs. Waggaman, lamenting the loss, poured out to her daughter tales of the family's financial embarrassment.[7]

Christine and her 'high lord' were hardly settled into married life in Cornwall when constitutional change and a general election thrust Sandfield permanently into public life. On 11 February 1841 Upper and Lower Canada were united into one province, each former unit, now section, securing equal representation in the new assembly and preserving many of its old distinctive features. The union, a modified implementation of a principal recommendation of Lord Durham's report of 1839, was in part a British device to solve Canadian unrest by absorbing the French Canadians in a future English-speaking majority. Colonel Alexander Fraser and John McGillivray, the two prominent political and social leaders or patrons of Glengarry, selected John Sandfield Macdonald, trained by the tory McLean and the moderate Draper, as their man to retain the county constituency for progressive, moderate, loyal conservatism.

Glengarry society and politics were still hierarchical, as to a lesser degree were most of the eastern counties of Upper Canada. Tone and style were set by the local semi-squirarchy whose influence in the East-

6 Waggaman Papers, in the possession of Mrs Quita Brodhead, Wayne, Pa., 19 Oct. 1841.
7 Langlois Papers, in the possession of Mrs. J. C. Brodie, Combermere, Ont., letter of 21 June 1843.

ern District was increased by Scottish clan traditions and by their ties with the élite in Toronto or Montreal. Fraser and McGillivray, both Highland-born and close friends, were well suited to deliver the Glengarry vote to Sandfield. Colonel Fraser held court at a huge stone mansion on his estate at Fraserville. Member of the legislative council and married to a granddaughter of Colonel John Macdonell (Leek), one of the foremost Loyalist chieftains, he was clearly the seigneur of the Catholic Scots, yet he kept close contact with Presbyterian interests by intimate correspondence with the Rev. John McKenzie of Williamstown. McGillivray, the junior patron, had settled in the county only after the absorption in 1821 of the North-West Company by the rival Hudson's Bay Company. Previously he had made a fortune from furs and had served the former company outside Canada on such remote rivers as the Peace and Athabasca. Soon after he settled in Glengarry and married Archibald McLean's sister, another granddaughter of John Macdonell, he became deeply engaged in real estate and assumed a position of leadership, serving for a time as provincial commissioner of crown lands and then as legislative councillor.

The result of the local election was never really in doubt. The suspicion that even moderate Reformers played into the hands of radicals who represented the insidious influence of republican America effectively killed the cause of Reform in the District, except in Dundas. Open voting took place throughout business hours in the week of 14 March. When polls closed on Friday night, Sandfield, who had not felt the need to deliver a single major address to the electors, was ahead 443 votes to 125 for Dr James Grant, the Reformer. Final voting on Saturday did not affect the trend.

The election nevertheless presented young John Sandfield with a serious problem. Union had bitterly divided Conservatives in the Eastern District. Fraser and McGillivray sided with the moderates of Upper Canada who suported Governor General Poulett Thomson and Attorney General Draper with their plan of union. On the other hand, the Stormont-Cornwall patrons, including Alexander McLean, Archibald's brother, had identified themselves with the now threatened Family Compact and therefore sided with the old-line tories who opposed the union as dangerous to Upper Canada and to the English interest. Sandfield was indeed caught in what was almost a fratricidal struggle. Though a former student of Archibald McLean, he was the nominee of Fraser, McGillivray and indeed Draper himself, and he enjoyed the support of the *Observer*, the moderate conservative Cornwall weekly.

Provincially Sandfield was regarded as a Draper Conservative. In congratulating the new member from Glengarry, Draper hinted at future favours and warned him to beware of all 'ultra' parties whether tory or radical and of certain individuals whom he left 'nameless' but who obviously were led by his own Solicitor General Robert Baldwin. 'Ponder this well,' he wrote to Sandfield, 'and make as I do the first question on every political dogma advanced no matter by whom, what will its effect be on the British Connexion.'[8] Rejected by Reformers yet mistrusted by old-line tories, Draper was trying vainly to hold together for Thomson, now Lord Sydenham, a coalition executive council which might safely launch the new ship of state.

During the first session of parliament, held in Kingston, Sandfield at times seemed strangely to be siding with his Stormont colleague, Alexander McLean, rather than his tutor Draper, but he never joined the old-line or right-wing tory caucus. This peculiar behaviour was a reaction against that part of the Sydenham-Draper reform program which, by threatening the old patronage system in the Eastern District, threatened Colonel Fraser and tended to reunite the Frasers and the McLeans. So Sandfield in the lower house and Fraser in the upper house tried vainly to stop the municipal bill which provided for elected district councils to replace the old courts of quarter sessions dominated by the justices of the peace, that is by the local patrons. With the tories they also opposed Draper's bill providing for easier naturalization of Americans. Although married to an American, Sandfield argued that it was easier to make the Niagara flow upstream than to make most Yankees into 'good subjects of this province.'[9] But then the aristocratic Waggamans and the Armaults were not Yankees.

Only part of Sandfield's attention could be devoted to provincial politics. Just before the session opened, he had been made president of the elected Cornwall board of police, the nearest equivalent to the office of mayor. Then on 11 August, Christine gave birth to a fragile

8 JSM Papers, 25 March 1841.
9 *Examiner* (Toronto), 11 Aug. 1841.

son, and Sandfield several times hurried home to be with his wife. The boy died in September, the same month Lord Sydenham died from a riding accident.

Draper lost no time in placating Fraser and Sandfield. He had Fraser appointed as the first warden of the Eastern District, a new post created by the municipal bill and one he held until 1850. This facilitated the transfer from the old system to the new. Besides, Fraser had been pleased with his continued influence in the election of the first district council. Fraser's position secure, Sandfield had the honour of delivering the speech of loyal welcome[10] when Sir Charles Bagot, the new governor general, first visited the area; he also had the privilege of seconding, when the legislature met in September 1842, the address-in-reply to Bagot's speech from the throne.

Ironically, Sandfield was no sooner comfortably re-established as a government supporter when the government changed. The strength and esprit of both the Lower and the Upper Canadian Reform opposition had grown, while Conservative bickering increased. With Draper's concurrence and resignation, Bagot replaced all but one minor Conservative in his council by Louis H. Lafontaine, the leader of the French-Canadian bloc, and Baldwin, A. N. Morin and two other Reformers. Francis Hincks, former Reform editor of the Toronto *Examiner*, had already become Inspector General. Sandfield had been impressed with Bagot and the collective action of his council. He saw no shift of policy coming from the change in personnel; he was also piqued by the attacks of the old-line tories on him personally for allegedly deserting them, when he had never in fact considered himself one of them. They had made, he told McGillivray, Draper's coalition untenable.[11] Although the former fur trader, who was no longer a legislative councillor, was upset by his support of the new alignment, Sandfield placated him by helping him with several urgent and valuable legal matters connected with his multifarious real estate. Fraser was less upset, because his interests were primarily local and were often related to having someone close to the government who would listen. For the first time in history, that government would be Reform-oriented. Fraser had long been concerned with obtaining for his beloved Glengarrians the best educational facilities possible, and Sand-

10 JSM Papers.
11 PAC, McGillivray Papers, 15 Sept. 1942.

field now secured a generous provincial grant for district education. Henceforth Fraser rarely attended the upper house.

Glengarry's coterie of old Reformers seemed more upset by Sandfield's position than did his supporters. Dr Grant complained to Baldwin that Fraser, 'of Tory memory,' and Sandfield were keeping their supporters on canal and other jobs despite the change of government.[12] Baldwin ignored Grant, and in November had Bagot promote Sandfield to the rank of lieutenant colonel in the 4th regiment of the Glengarry militia. Besides, John Sandfield's brother, Donald Alexander, secured the contract to build two sections of the Beauharnois plank road. Under the new system, Colonel J. S. Macdonald was quickly transforming his position in Glengarry from that of servant to that of master. In Cornwall, social life and entertaining at the Macdonald residence were increasing; bagpipes at parties, the rough Gaelic and vast quantities of strong drink mixed incongruously with the soft French tongue of the lovely Christine. But her activities were somewhat curtailed by her pregnancy and the birth on 3 October of a healthy daughter christened Lilla.

Then, in November 1843, Sandfield's political fortunes took an unexpected turn when all the Reformers in the executive council resigned following serious disagreement over control of patronage with Sir Charles Metcalfe, the new governor general; Metcalfe, backed by the British government, rejected the drift toward responsible government. Sandfield now took the final step in his political liberation. He permanently committed himself to being a Baldwinite Reformer; he rejected the position taken by Metcalfe and moved into opposition against an interim Conservative executive council headed by his former tutor Draper. When an election was finally called in the autumn of 1844, Sandfield was faced with a difficult task. Metcalfe, Draper and the Conservatives, backed enthusiastically by the Rev. Egerton Ryerson, the powerful Methodist leader, sought in Upper Canada to monopolize loyalty. Although Lafontaine swept Lower Canada despite Draper's earnest efforts to broaden his base to include prominent French Canadians, the government won overwhelmingly in Upper Canada. Nevertheless, backed by the Catholic clergy, Sandfield came off handsomely in Glengarry against Dr Grant, who ran as an independent Reformer with tory backing; he was also able to help defeat

12 Metropolitan Toronto Central Library, Robert Baldwin Papers, 4 Feb. 1843.

McLean in Stormont. Because the Conservative *Observer* now opposed Sandfield the Reformer, he had hired an editor for a temporary weekly called the *Freeholder*, which espoused the British connection, 'Liberal principles' and John Sandfield Macdonald.

Throughout the sessions of the second parliament, in Montreal, Sandfield worked faithfully and closely with Robert Baldwin. Letters indicate that he became his leader's chief agent in the eastern marches of Upper Canada, and he played a major role in the selection of candidates for the December 1847 election. Agreeing with Baldwin and over old Colonel Fraser's objections, he opposed Draper's moderate, and unsuccessful, university bill which would have established a federated Upper Canadian university made up of provincially endowed denominational colleges. Like Baldwin, Sandfield opposed segregating students on the basis of religion. In Glengarry, Scottish Catholics and Scottish Presbyterians went to the same school. Besides, Sandfield was a highly secular man. Christine was devout and the Macdonalds were generous financial supporters of Cornwall's St Columban's Church – they donated the parish bell – but John Sandfield himself rarely attended mass.

These were happy years for the Macdonalds. The tall, sophisticated Christine with her dark hair, large, dark, penetrating but soft eyes, graceful figure and long active fingers was a devoted wife, conscientious mother and popular hostess. John's political duties were not onerous, his legal business was expanding with astonishing rapidity, he was acquiring property, and he was developing solid financial independence. Economic difficulties would never be a problem for the once humble lad from St Raphael's. Christine gave birth to a second daughter, Mary Josephine, in November 1844, and to a third, Louise Christine, in August 1846. Her ties with her Louisiana family continued, and the christening of Louise was graced by the presence of her brother and sister, Eugene and Matilda.

With confidence Sandfield faced the elections, called by Governor General Lord Elgin. In Cornwall, Sandfield re-established his weekly *Freeholder* on a permanent foundation to fight his causes. Elgin and Lord Grey, secretary of state for the colonies, favoured responsible government. The ever loyal and beleaguered Draper had finally escaped to the bench, and Conservatives were destroying their party with fratricidal strife. The tide was running to Reform. Admittedly, minor difficulties which could later become serious for him appeared. In a moment of pique, Colonel Fraser voted against his protégé. Under Bishop Phelan of Kingston the Catholic hierarchy was passing from moderate Scottish to more conservative Irish hands; the bishop virtually called on the faithful to vote for the government even though the three Reform candidates in the Cornwall area were Catholics while the Conservatives were Presbyterian or Anglican. Sandfield's own opponent, Sheriff Alexander McMartin, was a respected veteran Conservative assemblyman. Sandfield won handsomely, but McMartin's candidacy forced him to work harder in Glengarry; he could not prevent McLean's re-conquest of Stormont and a bitterly fought Conservative victory in Cornwall. Baldwin was satisfied that these losses were more than compensated by other St Lawrence and Ottawa victories in which Sandfield had assisted. Provincially, the Conservatives had been routed; the Reformers had won a double majority. In congratulating Sandfield, Baldwin urged restraint and modest expectation; the impatience and dogmatism of their 'oversanguine friends,' he argued, could spell disaster.[13]

Reform power greatly increased Sandfield's influence. Formal responsible government was at hand. On 10 March 1848, Lafontaine, descendant of the conquered, became attorney general east and the first genuine premier of Canada. The Durham-Whig plan to absorb the French had been abandoned. Baldwin took charge, as Lafontaine's associate and attorney general west, of the Upper Canadian section of the cabinet. Sandfield used Reform patronage as a legitimate device to sustain his position and to extend his influence in the Eastern District and into the Ottawa valley. He admonished Inspector General Hincks that although nominations for minor offices might seem trivial compared with great matters of state, he could accept no delays or interference with appointments. The warning proved effective.[14] Throughout the area Sandfield tied the public careers of many lock masters, postal clerks and land officers to the career of the member from Glengarry. When in 1849 legislation abolished the districts and established self-government at the county level, Sandfield prevented the disruption of the Eastern District. To this day it survives as the 'United Counties of Stormont, Dundas and Glengarry.' After tory

13 JSM Papers, 1 Feb. 1848.
14 *Ibid.*, 12 Sept. 1848 and Hincks to JSM, 18 Sept. 1848.

youths rioted and burned the Montreal parliament buildings in April, Fraser made a rare appearance in the upper chamber, meeting in the Bonsecours Market Hall. He attacked the 'disastrous advice' tendered His Excellency over the Rebellion Losses Bill, but Sandfield was hardly worried. Sandfield not Fraser controlled Glengarry; Sandfield's *Freeholder* praised Elgin's grasp of responsible government; the Toronto *Globe*, now the Reform organ, reported a meeting of 1,200 loyal Glengarrians, as 'sound as ever,' ready to march for crown and governor against the Montreal tory rioters just as they had nine years earlier marched against Papineau's radical rebels.[15]

Sandfield also moved ahead at the provincial level. On 14 December 1849 Elgin on Baldwin's advice made him solicitor general west. This post was part of the ministry but not the cabinet and had been vacant for two months, since the elevation of William Hume Blake to the office of chancellor of the court of chancery. Baldwin, committed to the concept of equity, had secured reorganization and expansion of the court, but Sandfield had grave reservations about enlarging its scope. Five years previously he had had a personal scrape with the old court through the claims of some Cornwall tories that he had exercised undue influence in securing two town lots at deflated prices. The case had been dropped only to have Conservatives revive rumours during discussion of reorganization. Sandfield's misgivings about chancery and the rumours of scandal both contributed to a delay on Baldwin's part in offering him the vacant post. When Hincks too expressed misgivings yet boldly criticized his chief for fanning rumour by his tardiness, a piqued Baldwin abruptly issued the invitation. Sandfield thus became chief administrative assistant to Attorney General Baldwin. He was also made a queen's counsel. As was then the custom for appointees to the ministry, Sandfield had to resign his seat in the assembly. Re-elected by acclamation, he was escorted from Glengarry into Cornwall 'by scores of sleighs from the town itself, with flags flying and pipers playing'; later at a testimonial dinner attended by 100 guests, both 'Whig and Tory,' he referred to himself proudly as a former 'poor Glengarry boy.'[16]

Everywhere for Sandfield, matters were progressing splendidly. Or

15 *Globe* (Toronto), 12 May 1849.
16 Baldwin Papers, JSM to Baldwin, 12 Jan. 1850, and the *Globe*, 7 Feb. 1850.

11 September 1848 Christine had given birth to a hearty son, Henry Sandfield. The family moved permanently into Ivy Hall, a stately brick residence on the corner of York and Water streets that had once housed the imperial garrison. Situated across the street from the canal, the new home in summer provided an excellent view of steamships plying westward into the interior. John Sandfield's legal business, increasingly lucrative, now required the services of two assistants, John Walker and A. M. MacKenzie. Walker, who was becoming a compulsive drinker, lived at Ivy Hall and acted as family steward in the absence of the master. Both men kept their chief informed on political matters. The firm was being retained by a growing number of leading merchants in Montreal for the collection of local debts and other business. The practice also concerned itself with real estate transactions, wills and a few criminal cases, in fact the whole gamut of legal business in a small commercial town quickly leaving its pioneer era behind. In 1850 these commitments forced Sandfield to ask Baldwin for a short leave-of-absence. 'No barrister in Upper Canada,' wrote the *Globe*, 'stands higher in the estimation of mercantile men.'[17]

Not only were personal and business affairs going well but his political authority in the area was still increasing. Running himself for the Charlottenburg council, he and his candidates had won a great victory in the 1850 municipal elections. At its first meeting, the counties council chose as the first counties warden, Sandfield's close friend and confidant Dr Daniel E. McIntyre, a son-in-law of Colonel Fraser, the outgoing district warden. A few months later McIntyre secured appointment as counties sheriff, a post he held until his death in 1896; for years, this Church of Scotland sheriff acted as Sandfield's chief political agent and trouble shooter.

Although fortune shone for Sandfield in the eastern marches, the old Reform party of Upper Canada was in serious trouble, trouble which Sandfield could not ultimately escape. Factionalism, which had brought ruin to Upper Canadian Conservatism, was about to wreak havoc on Reform. It would carry Sandfield Macdonald into the political wilderness for eleven years. Radicals, both old men and young hot heads, were deeply dissatisfied with the pace of reform. It had slowly dawned on them that the aristocratic Baldwin and his Gallic twin were really quite conservative gentlemen. Neither was a demo-

17 9 Oct. 1849.

crat, favourably disposed toward manhood suffrage, and a wide extension of the elective principle. Furthermore, though Baldwin personally favoured the separation of church and state, he had compromised through Francis Hincks and Dr Egerton Ryerson, who since 1844 had been the chief superintendent of public instruction, in allowing provision for separate schools in the forward-looking Upper Canadian Common School Act of 1850. The act had provided for the establishment, on local option, of free elementary education, with half the funds coming from a provincial grant and the other half from local rates. But section 19, as finally passed, allowed twelve minority householders (Catholic or Protestant) the right to establish a provincially supported separate school where the common school teacher was not of the minority's faith. Meanwhile, with Lafontaine temporizing on the abolition of seigneurial tenure, Baldwin gave signs of the same tendency on the clergy reserves. Both leaders seemed too concerned about the prescriptive rights of property. In early 1850 the radicals had held conventions in Toronto and Markham and had founded virtually a separate democratic reform party which had as its organ the newly established Toronto *North American*, edited by William McDougall. Both friends and bitter critics such as Brown's *Globe* were soon calling the dissidents the Clear Grits.

But other forces were at work exacerbating the Reform difficulties, which although centred around Toronto and the Western Peninsula reached eastward into Sandfield's more traditionally oriented United Counties. One was the doctrinaire and puritanical Free Kirk movement which had disrupted Scottish Presbyterianism and now had George Brown as its chief spokesman in Upper Canada. Brown and the Free Kirkers were violently against any ties whatever between church and state. They and many other Protestants also bitterly opposed the growing force of the Tractarian, Anglo-Catholic or High Church movement among many tory Anglicans. The Clear Grits denounced both Tractarianism and the Catholic influence. Pope Pius IX's action in giving Cardinal Wiseman the title of Archbishop of Westminster and also giving other English prelates territorial titles seemed to many to symbolize the growing militancy and exclusiveness of Catholicism now led in Upper Canada by Irish immigrants and, ironically, an ultramontane French aristocrat, Bishop de Charbonnel of Toronto. The *Globe*, which continued to denounce Clear Grit democracy, hesitated, and then, beginning in late December 1851, like the radicals, it, too, became resolutely anti-Catholic. With all this animosity, Sheriff McIntyre reported to the member from Glengarry the growing social disruption reaching into the back concessions.[18] Old Dr Grant was thundering for the radicals in Stormont. Free Kirker A. M. McKenzie, employed by Sandfield and also local subscription agent for the *Globe*, candidly informed Sandfield that both Catholicism and Tractarianism had to be stopped.[19]

Sandfiield's own position became precarious when the provincial dissension proved more than the aloof Baldwin could bear. The final straw came when numerous Upper Canadian Reform lawyers along with the Conservatives supported an unsuccessful motion by the old rebel W. L. Mackenzie to abolish Baldwin's cherished court of chancery. Baldwin announced his retirement in favour of Francis Hincks. On 3 July, the day after Baldwin's announcement, the *Globe* came out resolutely for pressing forward with major reform and against both the government and the Clear Grits. Premier Lafontaine would also quit, dedicated as he was both to his retiring friend and to the principle that governments in Canada should command the support of majorities from both sections of the province: Mackenzie's mischievous motion had been defeated by only a Lower Canadian majority. Morin would be the new French-Canadian leader. What would happen to Sandfield Macdonald? He believed that he had a claim on the attorney generalship and rumours of his appointment to Baldwin's office grew. But Hincks distrusted the Glengarrian, considered him too independent, too close to the Clear Grits and to Brown, no longer popular with the Irish Catholic hierarchy, and not devoted to chancery. Besides, Hincks had decided to try to quiet the Clear Grits with a cabinet post. Unsuspectingly, Sandfield acted as go-between for Hincks to the Clear Grits, who demanded two seats in the cabinet and a shift in policy. Meanwhile Hincks secretly offered the attorney generalship to W. B. Richards, a quiet man who would give the premier unquestioned loyalty. He then acceded to the radicals' demands, thus filling the last cabinet posts he had available. In a condescending and supercilious letter on 11 October, the premier now urged Sandfield to remain solicitor general and blamed him for causing the radi-

18 JSM Papers, 8 June 1851.
19 *Ibid.*, numerous letters from 30 March to 26 June 1851.

cals to demand two seats.[20] Sandfield declined to answer the letter and resigned. Claiming that Hincks had let him out 'to pasture like an old horse,' he determined 'to pay him off.'[21] The insult was never forgotten or forgiven; eighteen years later it would return to haunt him in the twilight of his career.

Sandfield Macdonald thus became a frustrated independent Reformer. Yet in the December elections he secured his greatest regional triumph, returning to the Assembly with a considerable 'tail.' Glengarry re-elected him by acclamation. Sympathetic Reformers won the other three seats in the United Counties, and two or three neighbouring victors also seemed inclined toward him. Provincially, Hincks and Morin each secured majorities. In both sections, however, effectiveness depended on keeping the radicals in check. In Upper Canada, Brown and W. L. Mackenzie were also elected as independent Reformers. In Lower Canada, L. J. Papineau re-entered politics with a small coterie of opposition radicals or Rouges.

Francis Hincks and factionalism stemming from social and religious upheaval had together checked the political advance of John Sandfield Macdonald. Isolated from the centre of power, an embittered Sandfield took consolation in the size of his 'tail,' in his lucrative law practice and in the familial happiness and festivity of Ivy Hall.

20 *Ibid.* Hincks's version is in his *Reminiscences* (Toronto 1884), pp. 250–58.
21 JSM Papers, JSM to Edward J. Barker, 27 Dec. 1851, and Ontario, Dept. of Public Records and Archives (henceforth PAO), W. L. Mackenzie–Charles Lindsay Papers, JSM to Lindsay, 10 Jan. 1852.

2

Responsible Government with Irresponsible Ministers

The Canadian economy from 1852 to 1858 generally experienced unprecedented prosperity amid the great railway and wheat boom, but Canadian society became increasingly racked with bitter sectional and religious squabbling. For John Sandfield Macdonald these were six long years of political frustration.

The fact that Sandfield had emerged from the election with a rather long tail worried Premier Hincks. To mollify both he offered the speakership to the Glengarrian. Delaying for several months, aware that it was probably proffered as a 'douceur,' Sandfield finally accepted. In a long black gown over his long lean figure, with tricornered hat, white kid gloves, and a huge ring circling a gloved finger, and speaking the province's second language 'tolerably well,' he was an impressive champion of the Canadian commons, meeting now in the cliffed old capital of Quebec.[1] He clearly mastered his procedural duties and won the unstinting praise of Lord Elgin. Mixing the Gaelic, the English and the French, he and his wife were also perfect hosts and gala entertainers. At first Sandfield's local supporters were proud of his performance, but in time it occurred to many that the speakership was effectively muting the representation from the United Counties, at a time when the actions and especially the inaction of this most peculiar government were annoying the voters.

Around Cornwall and Glengarry the government's religious and

1 Mackenzie–Lindsay Papers, Henry Smith to Charles Lindsay, 2 April 1859, and JSM Papers, JSM to Edward J. Barker, 27 Dec. 1851.

educational policy was particularly unpalatable. Even the Clear Grits in the cabinet could accomplish little. Vestiges of the Anglican preferment remained. Moving too slowly on the clergy reserves, the government had merely asked Britain for permission to settle itself that anachronistic dispute and seemed paralysed when the permission was surprisingly granted. Meanwhile, the 'unprincipled Hincks' with the backing of Richards and Ryerson modified Baldwin's centralized and secular University of Toronto by creating University College as the teaching unit and providing for the affiliation and possible financial encouragement of the 'dirty sectarian colleges.'[2] A supplementary Upper Canadian education act, passed without an Upper Canadian majority, extended the rights of separate schools by exempting most separate school property holders from paying the local school rates. Finally, the premier was facilitating the passage of ecclesiastical corporation measures mainly affecting Lower Canada which Sheriff McIntyre and others condemned as 'religious Immaculate Conception' bills.[3] Sandfield's co-religionists, the Scottish Catholics, making up half of the 17,600 inhabitants of Glengarry (of whom 14,000 were Canadian-born and over 3,000 had the surname Macdonell or Macdonald), were disinclined to participate in the new aggressive and conservative mood sweeping European and Canadian Catholicism. Seeing no need for separate schools, they were attracted by the appeal of religious voluntarism. Among Free Kirkers and other evangelicals, George Brown's position was particularly popular. On motion from Sandfield's brother, Reeve Donald Alexander of Kenyon Township, a man who had no use for 'papists' or 'bigots' and who saw the church mainly as 'humbug,' the counties council passed unanimously a resolution condemning the new University Act. Donald also publicly and bitterly denounced Bishop Phelan and the Irish for attempting to promote sectarian education.[4] Nothing but subservience could be expected of 'Irish and French Papists,' volunteered the Free Kirker A. M .MacKenzie, 'but Scotsmen will not submit to be Priest-ridden.'[5] Donald agreed. 'His Holiness,' he wrote of Phelan, had had the auda-

2 JSM Papers, Donald Alexander Macdonald (henceforth DAM) to JSM, 15 March 1853.
3 *Ibid.*, McIntyre to JSM, 18 March 1853.
4 *Ibid.*, A. M. MacKenzie (henceforth AMM) to JSM, 9 Oct. 1852, and DAM to JSM, 5 April 1853.
5 *Ibid.*, AMM to JSM, 31 March 1853.

city to send up to Alexandria, the village Donald had established and now dominated, a new priest who must have been pulled out of 'some hole in Galloway.'[6] In June 1853, the Gavazzi riots further aggravated religious animosity; in Montreal, troops firing into the crowd on orders from the Irish Catholic mayor, who was a close friend of Hincks, killed nine Protestants as they were leaving Zion Church after hearing the renegade Italian priest preach.

Sandfield's advisers, Walker, MacKenzie, Sheriff McIntyre and Donald Alexander, all warned that he would be in serious trouble if he did not extricate himself from identification with cabinet ministers who were 'traitors to their avowed principles.'[7] Hincks and his followers, as the cowardly tools of the Irish hierarchy, were trying their hand at 'wooling' the electorate. This identification, they argued, had already doomed most of his tail.

But religious matters were not the only questions turning Sandfield's supporters and Reformers generally against the government. The premier's main concern was railways. The iron horse was indeed about to change the face of Canada, to reduce distances and bring divergent communities closer together for both cooperation and conflict. Parliament established a municipal loan fund to provide backing for local investment in railway promotion. It also passed the long-awaited Grand Trunk Railway Act creating a huge private British-controlled company, with massive assistance from Canadian public funds. Suspicion and dissatisfaction mounted when it was learned that six of the twelve Canadian directors were part of the ministry. The premier was one, and Solicitor General John Ross was the company's president. Glengarry promoters (of whom Sandfield's brother Donald was probably the chief) and farmers were critical of the fact that construction contracts were going to Englishmen. They were also unable to secure backing from Hincks for a railroad to Bytown from Montreal via Alexandria. Donald had planned to involve his brother in the purchase of a lumber company which would develop the back country north of Alexandria to be serviced by the Glengarry line.[8] Ranald Sandfield, who lived on the front in Lancaster and who believed that his younger brother Donald was himself partly to blame for political

6 *Ibid.*, DAM to JSM, 5 April 1853.
7 *Ibid.*, AMM to JSM, 2 March 1853.
8 *Ibid.*, DAM to JSM, 5 March, 5 and 8 April 1853.

disaffection in the back country, nevertheless warned his brother John that he dared not regard it lightly.[9]

Furthermore, the Representation Act of 1853 increasing the size of the assembly to 130 (65 for each section) from 84, and moving toward representation by population within each section, left the United Counties untouched and therefore weakened. Apart from this aspect, Sandfield and his friends liked the bill, and Ranald admitted that eastern Upper Canada had to face the hard fact that the Western Peninsula was undergoing phenomenal growth,[10] yet Glengarrians were bitter that in local terms their own county was under-represented. They were further annoyed when Attorney General Richards went to the bench to be succeeded by the president of the Grand Trunk, John Ross, a member of what McIntyre called the 'Irish-Toronto clique,' and not by their Sandfield.[11] Councillor Ross made no move to find a seat in the Assembly. Glengarrians were outraged by a proliferation of scandals. It appeared that the premier, in league with the mayor of Toronto, had netted £10,000 in a public land deal. 'What in the name of Heaven are we coming to as a party,' wrote William McDougall as his *North American* castigated the government despite its two Clear Grit 'prisoners.'[12] But even for many who were not radicals, the old Reform party no longer represented reform.

The speakership, it was clear, could offer Sandfield no sanctuary from the strong forces disrupting the party. But his private responsibilities prevented him from facing the problem squarely. His business affairs were going well, but they demanded much of his time. He was buying, selling and leasing much land, and in 1852 he obtained possession of a grist mill (Tombs Mills) and dam. The larger family was prospering. He had helped establish Ranald on his holding on the Lancaster front; although Ranald had caused the family worry with his eccentric living and his marriage outside the church to a girl of questionable behaviour, he proved to be stable. In Alexandria, where he held court and owned a general store and grist mill, Donald had become a successful entrepreneur. After his first wife had died, Donald had married Catherine Fraser, another daughter of the old

9 *Ibid.*, Ranald Sandfield Macdonald (henceforth RSM) to JSM, 26 March 1853.
10 *Ibid.*, RSM to JSM, 26 March and 1 April 1853.
11 *Ibid.*, McIntyre to JSM, 22 April 1853.
12 PAO, Charles Clarke Papers, McDougall to Clarke, 17 Sept. 1853.

colonel. More enterprising than brother John, he had already been involved in major contracts concerning the Illinois Canal, the Beauharnois Canal and road; he was now building a massive aquaduct for the Montreal water works. At Ivy Hall, just after the prorogation of parliament, Christine gave birth on 28 June 1853 to a third daughter, Adele. But for some time Sandfield's lungs had been giving him serious trouble; he had been ordered to seek a rest and a change. In July 1853 he undertook a six months' visit to Britain and the Continent. With the best medical help and relaxation, he seemed partly to recover, but for the rest of his life he would be a weak, sickly semi-invalid. In London, however, Sandfield had undertaken one piece of dubious business. He procured a sub-contract for his brothers to construct the Grand Trunk from Montreal to Farran's Point in western Stormont. McDougall of the *North American* estimated that the Sandfields stood to make about £60,000 on the deal.[13] If this had been meant as a government bribe, it failed dismally.

The legislative session of 1854, after long delays, finally opened on 13 June 1854. Speaker Sandfield was hard pressed to control from the chair the deadly assaults mounted on the treasury benches by both Conservatives, led by John A. Macdonald, and Reformers, led by George Brown and Louis V. Sicotte, an independent Reformer who had first suported Morin. With two amendments to the address in reply, the combined but disunited opposition defeated the government 42 to 29. The three members of Sandfield's tail from the United Counties all voted against the government. Hincks seemed finished. Despite the railway contract, Sandfield was about to extricate himself from a discredited régime headed by a man he detested. The greatest of good times, brought on by continued railway expansion, the Crimean war with Russia, growing wheat exports, and the British North American Reciprocity Treaty with the United States had not been able to paper over the huge cracks in Reform unity.

But Hincks was not yet finished. Two days after the vote, Sandfield and other members were astonished to hear the ceremonial sound of guns foretelling Lord Elgin's imminent visit to the legislative council. He was coming to dissolve parliament before it had accomplished a single item of business, before it had even finished the debate on the address. Uproar prevailed as Black Rod knocked at the door and re-

13 *Ibid.*, McDougall to Clarke, 4 April 1854.

quested members' presence in the upper house. Brown and John A. Macdonald roared their protests. Speaker Sandfield, however, with great deliberation and obvious displeasure, rose and left for the council chambers. It was one of those rare moments in modern British parliamentary practice when the constitutional procedures of the eighteenth and early nineteenth centuries were superseded by those of an earlier age. In the Canadian lords sat the late hero of responsible government, James Bruce, Earl of Elgin, like a Stuart monarch, and at the bar stood a proud and irate John Sandfield Macdonald, spokesman for the Canadian commons. Before the occupant of the throne could read the closing address, the speaker burst forth with a stern, proper and formal speech challenging the constitutionality of the proceedings. He noted that it had not been possible for him to fulfil the 'immemorial custom of a Speaker of the Commons House of Parliament' of loyally replying to 'your gracious Speech from the Throne' because of the irregular and uncustomary summoning which the Assembly had now received.[14] Then the speaker made the governor submit to something that neither James I nor his son had endured: slowly he repeated the entire speech in French. Elgin, who had started the bilingual tradition in 1848, was visibly enraged. Although prorogation and dissolution followed forthwith, it was one of Sandfield's greatest moments.

Overnight John Sandfield Macdonald became a popular hero. Before leaving Quebec City, Upper Canadian opposition Reformers met with him to plan their strategy. Brown was there, and so were some of the Clear Grit leaders. They determined to work for the overthrow of Hincks and for the reconstruction of a Reform administration under the premiership of their bold speaker. Brown later referred to Sandfield's leadership stemming in part from 'our compact at the breaking up of the house.' Sandfield, his followers and some Clear Grits also met over breakfast with Papineau, L. V. Sicotte and several of the Rouge backbenchers.[15] Shortly thereafter a 'large body' of Sandfield's admirers got up a subscription and engaged Théophile Hamel to prepare his portrait as the great defender of the rights of the people.

Sandfield had been fully aware of the responsibility he had under-

14 Canada, *Journals of the Legislative Assembly* (henceforth JLA), 1854, p. 31.

15 Queen's University, Alexander Mackenzie Papers, George Brown to JSM, 16 Aug. 1854; also, *Globe*, 28 June 1854.

taken by interrupting the governor and questioning the constitutionality of his actions. He instructed Alpheus Todd, the assistant legislative librarian and constitutional expert, to investigate the historical grounds for his challenge. The detailed report which Todd submitted cited precedents and analogies from Elizabethan, Stuart and even Hanoverian experience and 'amply vindicated' the speaker's behaviour.[16]

For both Sandfield and the county the election was inconclusive and confusing. Glengarry returned Sandfield by acclamation and his followers were victorious in Stormont and Cornwall, but the Conservatives made substantial gains throughout the eastern marches. Moderate Conservatives also made modest gains in western areas, where the *Globe* seemed to prefer them to Hincksites when no opposition Reformer was available. Brown sent a letter of congratulation to Sandfield, pledging his support for a régime under the premiership of the Glengarrian dedicated to the full separation of church and state and to representation by population. He urged Sandfield to draw in wavering Reformers, consort with Antoine-Aimé Dorion, the new Rouge leader, and Louis Sicotte in Lower Canada, and for tactical reasons to stand for re-election as speaker.[17]

Although Sandfield failed to do much consorting, he did join Brown in a post-election political tour of the west. These two affluent Scots made an incongruous Reform pair. The robust Brown was a deeply religious Free Kirker, the new voice of Toronto and the expanding west, an ardent journalist and reluctant politician; six years his elder, the ailing Sandfield, technically a Catholic, was a secularist in an age of religion, more 'Central Canadian' than Upper Canadian, a veteran politician and a casual newspaper owner. Brown was dogmatic; Sandfield tended toward pragmatism. Both men opposed corruption and the abandonment of Reform principles; both eschewed the democratic radicalism of the Clear Grits. Their inspiration was British not American, mercantile not agrarian. Both detested Hincks. Brown had opposed Sandfield's elevation to the speakership, but he had rejoiced in the continued tension between premier and speaker. Now, with Brown's help, Sandfield seemed on the verge of becoming premier and attorney general west.

It was not to be so. Morin had strengthened his hold on the Lower

16 JSM Papers, Todd to JSM, 6 July 1854, with enclosed brief.
17 Mackenzie Papers, Brown to JSM, 16 Aug. 1854.

Canadian majority. When parliament met on 5 September 1854, George-Etienne Cartier, Morin's candidate for speaker, lost but only by three votes. For reasons of prestige and not expecting a victory, the Rouges then put forth the name of Sicotte; with Sicotte's defeat, they would have supported Sandfield's candidature, one that would probably have received wide Conservative support. But during the voting on Sicotte, Hincks jumped up shouting 'Put me among the Ayes.' Sandfield allegedly growled an angry 'Thank you,' which was met by an ironical bow from the premier.[18] Morin and the government's supporters followed the premier, and Sicotte was elected. Nevertheless, the combined opposition soon defeated the government. On 8 September the Hincks–Morin ministry resigned. In making his explanation to the house, the outgoing premier attempted particularly to ridicule Sandfield by again recounting the official version of the cabinet negotiations of 1851.

Much to Sandfield's astonishment Elgin did not call on him; instead, Elgin asked his own tory critic, old Sir Allan MacNab, to attempt an administration. The premier-elect, with able assistance from John A. Macdonald and Francis Hincks, erected the McNab–Morin government and the 'Liberal–Conservative Coalition.' The Lower Canadian membership remained the same as before; its followers were soon being called Bleus. The Upper Canadian portion had three Conservatives, with John A. Macdonald in the coveted office of attorney general west, and two Hincksite Reformers, including John Ross of the Grand Trunk. Ross was also Baldwin's son-in-law, and the old chief, fearing the radical and republican tendencies of the Clear Grits, blessed the union. The new government would and did secularize the clergy reserves and provide for the extinction of seigneurial tenure. Shortly, the government was obtaining comfortable double majorities. The greatest reorganization of political forces in Canadian parliamentary history had just been accomplished.

Sandfield Macdonald, his 'tail,' George Brown, the Clear Grits, Wiliam Lyon Mackenzie, and the Rouges were all left isolated and wandering in the shades of opposition. Sandfield was titular leader of the opposition, but there was no united opposition to lead. He suffered the disadvantage of not having a large personal following, al-

18 J. A. Collins, *Life and Times of John A. Macdonald* (Toronto 1883), p. 177.

though a few of the former Hincksites who deserted the coalition, men such as Michael Foley of Waterloo North, seemed inclined to regard him as their chief. Another deterioration in Sandfield's health further weakened his effectiveness as leader. In November his chest trouble was so bad that he was confined to bed in Quebec City. 'It is reported all over here,' wrote the faithful sheriff, Dr. McIntyre, with unintended humour, 'that you are at death's door. Why do you not write me?'[19] Meanwhile, Brown's stature continued to grow. Ending the doctrinal feud, William McDougall sold the *North American* to the *Globe* in February 1855 and became an employee of his former rival. The radical strain of Clear Grittism which Brown abhorred survived, but the ubiquitous *Globe* temporarily blotted it out. Brown even accepted the word 'Grit.' Sandfield and Brown cooperated in attacking the government for perpetuating the worst features of the Hincks regime. Sandfield accused it of financial extravagance, jobbery and waste in various public works. Both men continued to oppose state aid to sectarian institutions, charitable or educational. 'Why should we vote money,' Sandfield said, 'to keep up these sectarian distinctions which now exist amongst us?'[20]

With Sandfield tied down in Quebec City, his opponents in Cornwall and Glengarry, ably assisted by the Irish hierarchy, were boiling up quite a brew. The Sandfield brothers were being attacked for their secularism.[21] Bishop Phelan was again trying to make the common school in Alexandria, where Donald was virtual laird, into a separate one or else establish a new separate school. For this purpose he had sent to the village another new priest, Father John McLachlan, who though an Aberdeen man, was dubbed 'Spanish John' because of his jesuitical tendencies. In 1854 Glengarry had 61 common schools and no separate ones, and the teacher in Alexandria was a Protestant. On Easter Sunday of that year, Spanish John had read from the pulpit a letter from the bishop exhorting Catholics to establish their own schools, and proceeded to preach on the subject. An incensed Donald

19 JSM Papers, 15 Nov. 1854.
20 *Globe*, 15 Dec. 1854.
21 The episode of the dispute in Glengarry has been pieced together from a multiude of sources: *True Witness and Catholic Chronicle* (Montreal), 27 Oct., 10 Nov. and 8 Dec. 1854; *Globe*, 18 Dec. 1854; JSM Papers, AMM to JSM, 17 Oct., 11, 24, 25 Nov., 4, 6, 7, 11, 15 Dec. 1854, RSM to JSM, 12 Nov. 1854, and DAM to JSM, 23 Nov. 1854.

had left his pew at the end of the service and harangued his village folk from the church doorway on the folly of segregated education. The next Sunday, McLachlan had preached against the absent 'petty miller' and untalented 'devil's agent' who had 'sprung from nothing ... like mushrooms on a dung hill.' The future lieutenant governor of Ontario thereupon had charged the priest in court with defamation of character. In November, the Irish-Catholic organ of Montreal, the *True Witness*, assisted by McLachlan, broadened the attack from Donald to the three elder Sandfield brothers and their religious liberalism. Before Judge Archibald McLean, Donald lost his suit. The previously reckless Ranald was worried, but he told John that it might check Donald's 'high notions' and teach him to be more judicious. McLachlan described the three Sandfields as 'no Catholics' at all and found a political challenger to the sitting member. He also arranged for the local distribution of the *True Witness* free from door to door. When meeting Protestants, many of John Sandfield's Catholic friends were deeply embarrassed. Alexander Francis Macdonald, John's aloof youngest brother who had almost entered the priesthood, tried resolutely to suppress the inflammatory issues. Reminding the Glengarrians of Culloden, the *True Witness* argued that the faithful could hardly vote again for such an apostate. Donald wrote back, boldly defending his educational position. The *True Witness* for a time refused to print the letter, but the Montreal *Herald* and the Cornwall Conservative *Constitutional* did. Thereupon Sandfield's legal assistant, A. M. MacKenzie, pitched in intemperately against the 'Spanish' influence. Donald wrote John that Phelan had even sent in 'prowling beggars,' or friars to help in the fight. Finally, just before Christmas, the weary and ailing opposition leader returned to Ivy Hall to take charge personally of the situation. His presence deflated the movement to raise up a political challenger, and the exuberant Donald was ordered to use more discretion. For most of that winter, however, relations between the two brothers remained strained.[22]

The 'Spanish influence' did not withdraw, but by March 1855 the tide had clearly turned in favour of the Sandfield brothers who had patched up their own differences. John Sandfield rejoiced that Donald, ironically, was able to play Joseph to 'Father McLachlan's friends' in late April and May during a lingering winter, one of the

22 *Ibid.*, RSM to JSM, 4 March 1855.

most severe on record. The miller of Alexandria had large quantities of hay to spare and gallantly dispersed to farmers and village folk the essentials for their hungry livestock.[23]

During the winter of 1854–5 Sandfield had also been forced to give serious attention to his own lucrative business affairs. His chief assistant, John Walker, was now an incorrigible alcoholic and a junior lawyer was little better. The abstemious MacKenzie was promoted to *de facto* steward – though during the spring of 1855 he announced long-range plans to set up his own business. Alcohol and the bar made a common mixture in little Cornwall; MacKenzie reported to Sandfield that it was not unusual to see barristers 'stretched out upon the street in a helpless state of intoxication.'[24] As steward, MacKenzie had also to superintend a complete overhaul of the troublesome and costly mill. Still, from the legal practice the funds continued to pour in; two accounts settled by MacKenzie just before Christmas 1854 netted over £400 each. In Cornwall's fall assizes for 1855, Sandfield and a temporarily behaving Walker were involved in 41 of the 61 cases; for 1856 the count would be 59 out of 70.

Meanwhile in parliament, during the 1855 session in Quebec and the 1856 session in Toronto, Sandfield's position slipped somewhat, and differences between himself and George Brown became more apparent. Sandfield declined to support Brown's lonely stand against making the upper house progressively elective, and he participated in none of the *Globe* editor's thunder against Lower Canada. Although the population of Upper Canada seemed to be outstripping that of Lower Canada, Sandfield did not back Brown's demand for representation by population. In all this Sandfield was encouraged by a growing number of Central Canadian correspondents who praised his moderation and warned him against over-identification with the Rouge extremists of Montreal and a doctrinaire stand on religious issues which could only hurt 'the feelings and influences of all liberal French-Canadian Roman Catholics.'[25] Like many other Reformers, Sandfield missed debate on and passage of the surprise separate school bill introduced late in the session of 1855 by Dr E. P. Taché, new leader of the Bleus. This measure, passed over Brown's objections and

23 *Ibid.*, DAM to JSM, 27 April 1855.
24 *Ibid.*, 25 Sept. 1855.
25 *Ibid.*, William Armstrong to JSM, 14 March 1855.

without an Upper Canadian majority, extended the rights of Upper Canadian separate school supporters. By the bill, any ten Catholic householders in a locality could vote to establish a school, elect trustees, share in the legislative grant, and so long as they kept their rates as high as the common school rates be exempt from paying those rates. Because he undoubtedly would have voted with Brown, it was unfortunate for their future relationship that Sandfield was inadvertently absent. Ramifications of the Taché act were later to affect profoundly the career of this secular Catholic.

In 1856 the opposition no longer recognized any official leader. Sandfield's clash with Brown that session came with the Glengarrian's championship of Lafontaine's principle of the double majority. It followed a particularly vicious reorganization of the cabinet, subsequent to its failure again to obtain an Upper Canadian majority in the assembly on a contentious division. The shuffle involved ditching Premier MacNab, and while Taché emerged as premier, the dominant force was John A. Macdonald. On 3 June Sandfield, seconded by C. J. Laberge, a leading Rouge, moved in favour of establishing the rule that cabinet members from each section should possess the confidence of a majority of the assemblymen from their section. Government should be supported by a double majority, a majority in each section. Without the principle's having secured recognition, it had, in effect, been practised since the achievement of responsible government. Premiers had resigned soon after they lost the confidence of one or other of the sections. Sandfield, erroneously, believed, furthermore, that Baldwin's retirement had been directly related to his loss of Upper Canadian majority support for his judicial program. In his speech on this motion, Sandfield claimed that the double majority was inherent in the Canadian operation of responsible government, given the sectional nature of the union of 1841 and the abandonment of Britain's policy of absorbing the French. Canada was a country of two peoples. 'Glengarry,' he argued, 'would be the last place to throw off the British connection, but she would respect no Governor who did not respect the constitutional rights of the people.' The simple majority now worked against Upper Canada, but, he warned, soliciting Lower Canadian support, in the future it would readily be used 'to carry measures which the Lower Canadians would not like.'[26] Sand-

26 *Globe*, 4 June 1856.

field was not surprised by John A.'s ridiculing of his speech as an academic 'historical essay' or by G.-E. Cartier's exhortation to the Bleus not to be tempted, but he was stunned and offended by the vehement attack launched by his colleague, George Brown. While castigating the government for misruling Upper Canada, Brown caused a 'sensation' by denouncing Sandfield's proposal as merely a novel 'bait' used to lure restless French Canadians. He accused Sandfield of promoting French-Canadian fears of representation by population and of ultimate Upper Canadian dominance, in order to promote 'a new political alliance,' perhaps a Sandfield-Bleu government. Sandfield leaped to his feet, burst into Brown's speech, and categorically denied any such plans. Brown replied that he hoped his warning would stop any 'unholy alliance,' that Sandfield should serve only in an administration with Dorion and 'other men of Liberal principles' currently in opposition; Reformers would soon sweep Upper Canada and rule the country with a single majority. Sandfield had argued that the double majority recognized and moderated sectionalism; Brown insisted that the double majority promoted sectionalism, a spirit of dualism which prevented Canadians from entering into their inheritance of 'half of this vast continent.'[27] Three core members of Sandfield's tail were absent when only fifteen votes were secured for the motion. The *Globe*, which unfairly called the double majority a vicious invention of the 'priest party,' was substantially correct when it pointed out that many who voted for the resolution, such as W. L. Mackenzie and some of the most radical Rouges, were really separatists who favoured the dissolution rather than the preservation of the union.[28]

Besides the anguish of renewed party division, Sandfield had to face serious deterioration of his health. Frequently confined to bed during the session of 1856, he had received best wishes from John A. who wrote, '*We want* you very much in the House.'[29] Later, at Ivy Hall, the tuberculosis worsened, and in December, on medical advice, he headed south for the winter. He visited with Waggaman relatives and friends, received treatment, and took a Caribbean cruise. Although he was home in the late spring, he attended the session of 1857 for less than a week. Henceforth he had the use of only one lung.

27 *Ibid.*, 5 June 1856.
28 *Ibid.*, 4 June 1856.
29 JSM Papers, 14 May 1856.

In November 1857, after the dissolution of parliament, he came to a major decision: the riding of Glengarry was too large and too demanding for him to represent. Instead, the robust and more aggressive Donald would handle Glengarry. He would take Cornwall which, while it had a less secure past, was small and not as onerous to service. He actually might gain by the transfer. Few associations would be lost, and Donald might learn the restraint that frequently comes from having responsibility. With less than 700 voters, Cornwall was almost a rotten borough; it could now be made into something approaching a pocket borough.

Working together, the Sandfield brothers achieved great success in the December election. By a vote of 1,556 to 246 Donald defeated the candidate of the 'Spanish party,' his brother-in-law Archibald Fraser who, ironically, was an Old Kirk Presbyterian. By a closer vote of 428 to 246, John defeated an old Tory notable, Philip Vankoughnet (whose son was in the cabinet). (Fifty years later, a Catholic clergyman asserted, without documentation, that John Sandfield had given some heed to an episcopally inspired delegation from Catholic St. Andrew's, a village north of the town but in the constituency, that he desist from opposing separate schools or lose their votes.[30]) Both Stormont and Dundas also went Reform as did a small majority of the seats throughout Upper Canada.

Perhaps Sandfield and the United Counties delegation held the key to survival for John A. Macdonald who, though now the premier, lacked majority support from his section. Certainly something had to be done. Brown's 'rep by pop' seemed irresistible. Besides, following the end of the Crimean war, the economic boom and inflation were giving way to depression. He needed a strong government. Early in 1858, the premier met and offered a cabinet position to the member for Cornwall. On a business trip to Montreal Sandfield let it be known that the offer had been made, that as a price for any further consideration of it he had demanded office for himself and three other Reformers. Acquiescence would have left John A. with only one other Conservative. When the premier finally countered with the offer of one other seat plus another post for a pro-government Hincksite,

30 George Corbet, *A Retrospect: First Catholic Diocese of Upper Canada and the Evolution of the Catholic School System* (Cornwall, *c.* 1917), pp. 65–66.

Sandfield wired laconically, 'No go.'[31] If he had been seriously tempted, which was doubtful, a family schism would have ensued. Donald assured George Brown that he himself would never go over 'with a brother or any other person.'[32] The premier had to make less satisfactory arrangements.

In opposition, Sandfield continued to be outclassed by Brown. The session of 1858 was preceded by a caucus of the combined opposition presided over by the *Globe* editor. Had it not been for Luther H. Holton, the brilliant Montreal financier who headed the English-speaking Liberal forces from Lower Canada, Brown would have totally ignored his former chief. With Holton as the link between Grits and Rouges, Brown was groping toward some formula, perhaps using centralized federalism, which would preserve the union, achieve 'rep by pop' and still win some minority support with the French. Holton reminded the impatient Brown that Sandfield was becoming popular with a growing body of restless Bleus attracted by the double majority and by his obvious understanding and appreciation of their culture and position.[33] But Brown and Sandfield, competing against one another with their proposed constitutional solutions, had to contend with a number of others: Dorion's advocacy of splitting the province into a loose two-state confederacy, various radicals' proposals of total separation, Alexander Galt's tight federation of all of British North America, and the unsatisfactory status quo maintained by Cartier and Macdonald.

On 19 May, 1858, Sandfield delivered, on his 'hobby,' what even the *Globe* had to admit was the best speech of his career.[34] Although adding nothing substantially to what he had said in 1856, he argued now with more lucidity, moderation and authority. Admitting that many of his colleagues still could not accept his viewpoint, he laid claim to patience. Having no particular love for office, he was willing to go on fighting for what he believed and, if necessary, to remain in opposition 'till the end of time.' On this occasion, he was backing a motion by J.-E. Thibaudeau, a restless Bleu, rather than speaking for one of his own, and he openly courted other Bleus, appealing to their

31 Macdonald Papers, Macdonald to JSM, 26 Jan. 1858, and JSM to Macdonald, 27 Jan. 1858.
32 PAC, Brown Papers, 27 Jan. 1858.
33 *Ibid.*, 2 Feb. 1858.
34 20 May 1858.

sense of fair play and their fears that some day the situation under Governor Metcalfe, when the French had had little influence, might return. The fabric of the Canadian union, a union imposed from without, had never been strong. Now economic trouble was added to the deepening centrifugation. The alleged dictation of Upper Canada by the Bleu-Catholic leadership led to radical Grit cries for dissolution, while the more moderate Grit demands for representation by population and the Calvinist proclivities of the *Globe* aroused in French Canadians the deepest fears for *la survivance*. Sandfield was convinced that the immediate way to preserve the deeply desirable union was to admit its duality and 're-establish' the principle of the double majority. For Sandfield, that principle was no permanent end in itself but rather a means of preserving the noble Canadian experiment, now extolled despite its peculiar origins by most thoughtful Canadians of both cultures.

At 2.15 AM on 20 July the Thibaudeau motion finally came to a vote; it lost 33 to 65 with Brown, Dorion and all the ministers opposing it. But it secured the backing of several prominent Bleus, including three ex-ministers, as well as Thomas D'Arcy McGee, the Montreal Liberal Irish leader, and Michael Foley and several other moderate Reformers from Upper Canada.

After surviving several votes by a thread, the government fell, 28 July, on a simple opposition amendment asserting that Ottawa ought not to become the capital – despite its being the Queen's so-called choice. George Brown impatiently accepted the premiership offered by Governor General Sir Edmund Head; Sandfield Macdonald hesitantly became attorney general west. Although Sandfield had not played a major role in the involved negotiations preceding the establishment of the Brown-Dorion Reform government, Holton had been right; his inclusion was essential. Alone, Brownites and Rouges had absolutely no hope of success; in fact, a majority in the ten-man cabinet, though it included Oliver Mowat and Holton, were neither. Besides Sandfield, the moderates included Foley, L. T. Drummond and Thibaudeau; five had supported the double majority. Nevertheless, with the ministers barred from the Assembly pending re-election, the government within two days was defeated 71 to 31. Head refused dissolution. With Cartier as premier and Galt as finance minister, the Conservatives returned to office, and, through a dubious device (the 'double shuffle' of ministerial offices), kept their seats without re-election.

Sandfield might better have declined to serve the Brown-Dorion government, even though he had been offered Baldwin's old portfolio. Its basic policy was too vague to allay fears. Brown was still anathema to French Canada and had insisted that representation by population be accepted as a goal; Dorion was later to claim that genuine federation and representation by population with iron-clad guarantees to French Canada were alternatives, whereas Brown saw federalism as the guarantee. Dorion also claimed later that implementation of the final constitutional form agreed upon would depend on prior acceptance by Sandfield's double majority. Yet had Sandfield remained aloof from this bizarre affair, he would have been blamed for its collapse. Sandfield, with his Montreal orientation, his sympathy for the French, his advocacy of political dualism and general moderation, was potentially acceptable to Lower Canada. Yet particularism, sectionalism and sectarianism and his own poor health had severely weakened his position in Upper Canada. At the moment it was not plausible for him to endeavour to assert leadership over a reunited Baldwinite Reform party.

3

The Baldwinites and the Mauves

Until almost the end of 1858, a kind of angry buoyancy sustained the spirits of the 'immortal twelve' (the ten of the cabinet and the two solicitors general) who had made up 'Her Majesty's Most Ephemeral Government.' Sandfield joined his colleagues and D'Arcy McGee in a series of popular cross-Canada banquets to extol their cause and to denounce the arbitrary action of the governor, whose principles, wrote the *Globe*, had 'once cost an English king his head and should now cost this Head his office.'[1] But Sandfield believed that Brown's impatience to seize office had been the chief cause of the fall; he, therefore, resented the adulation poured on the erstwhile premier. 'Can't you do anything without George Brown,' he barked one evening from his carriage to Charles Clarke, the doughty Elora Grit who was hosting the local banquet and showing his deep displeasure at Brown's unexpected absence.[2] In December, Chief Justice Draper sustained the ministers on the legality of the double shuffle. Reform morale, particularly Grit morale, sank. Sandfield himself took some consolation from the resignation from the ministry on Christmas Eve of Louis Sicotte. After serving as speaker, Sicotte had joined the cabinet late in 1857. Always restless under Cartier, this St Hyacinthe maverick quit because the premier refused to consider the 28 July vote as a meaningful repudiation of Ottawa as capital. Around Sicotte,

1 6 Aug. 1858.
2 Charles Clarke, *Sixty Years in Upper Canada* (Toronto 1908), pp. 138–39.

Thibaudeau and other friends in Lower Canada, Sandfield would encourage the development of an expanding group of Mauve Reformers with whom he and his Upper Canadian friends could cooperate to alleviate sectional dissension and try to restore Reform ascendancy. The government could be vulnerable to a sustained, united Reform assault. Despite the Draper decision, that government was reeling under deepening economic distress, Bleu unrest and a severe rebuff from the colonial office for its Galt-inspired proposal for British North American union.

During the session of 1859, Reformers were, however, anything but united. Sandfield clashed head on with Brown over the principle of Canadian unity versus Upper Canadian rights. Although neither man was guilty of duplicity, both disputed intemperately. The specific occasion was a complicated government bill to implement the report of a commission on the additional money necessary to extinguish claims of seigneurs for compensation for loss, under the act of 1854, of the casual dues from their former censitaires.[3] The issue was how the $3,250,000 was to be paid. The bill provided for gradual payment out of general revenue with proportional amounts set aside for the municipal loan funds for Upper Canada and the Eastern Townships. Sandfield voted against the bill, on the grounds that it severely extended coverage beyond the commitment of 1854 by including mortmain religious seigneuries in the generous compensation. Yet he did agree with Thibaudeau and many others in the Lower Canadian opposition that a Reform government would have employed virtually the same plan for payment, but applied only to lands covered by the act of 1854. Brown vehemently denied this; even though the censitaires could not have been charged directly, Upper Canadians would not have had to help extinguish the claims. An outraged Sandfield left the chamber during Brown's speech. He later claimed that Lower Canada, apart from the loan fund, had no separate monies and that a charge on the affected municipalities would have been the same as a charge on the censitaires. Seeing a sectional tax as politically suicidal, many Lower Canadian Reformers formally withdrew their support

3 The whole dispute is reviewed, with public letters and reprints of the debates, in the *London Free Press* (henceforth *LFP*), 4, 8, 10 and 19 July 1860; also note the *Leader* (Toronto), 16 April 1859, and the *Globe*, 9 and 10 April 1859.

from Brown. Sandfield for his part had only briefly attended one opposition caucus since the last general election. The position of leader of the opposition was thus again vacant. Brown later admitted to Holton how deeply indebted he was to Dorion's loyalty, yet the more he stood up to the Rouges, to say nothing of the Bleus, the greater he thought his western popularity would be.[4]

Sandfield and his French-Canadian friends had raised doubts about Brown's championship of Upper Canada. Sandfield emphasized a united but dual Canada centred on Montreal. For Brown, destiny favoured the progressive Toronto, whose evangelical Protestant entrepreneurs and their nearby yeoman customers were to look north up Yonge Street and the track of the Northern Railway, up beyond Fort William past the thousand miles of rocky wilderness to the fertile plains of the great Northwest, still partially locked in by a tired old mercantilist, beaver-oriented monolith. For Sandfield, expansion westward should await the establishment of amiable relations in the heartland. In this task Brown and the self-righteous Grits were divisive forces; 'Central Canadians,' located in the upper St Lawrence and Ottawa valleys, were the natural unifiers. For them, if anything external were attempted, it ought to be a railway to link Montreal with Halifax.

The argument over paying the seigneurs helped Sandfield find a deeply significant ally and friend in the very centre of the Grit-dominated peninsula.[5] This was Josiah Blackburn, owner and editor of the *Free Press* of London. In 1857 Blackburn had unsuccessfully contested the seat of Middlesex East for Reform. In 1858 his paper endorsed Sandfield's concept of the double majority, at least as an interim device. Later, it objected to the pathological stand which the *Globe* took over the Draper decision.[6] On the seigneurial question Blackburn was convinced by the arguments of Sandfield and the rest that Brown would indeed have agreed to place the burden for compensation on

4 Mackenzie Papers, Brown to Holton, 8 July 1859.

5 In the 1857 election, Reformers won 14 of the 20 seats from the 14 counties west of Wentworth. Four of the six Liberal-Conservative ridings were contiguous, extending from Elgin West through Middlesex East and London to Perth; in this area the Irish Protestant vote was strong. Of the other two, Essex had an unstable record; Waterloo South was Reform on all other occasions from 1854 to 1867. The Niagara peninsula divided four to four.

6 *LFP*, 7 Jan. 1858 and 20 and 23 Dec. 1859.

the general taxpayer. With considerable backing from other journals, the paper called Brown's integrity into question and claimed that Brownites only represented a minority of Upper Canadian Reformers.[7] Brown was a general 'upon whose banners the eagle of success never alights.'[8] Blackburn soon developed close personal contacts with Sandfield, a potential leader who held similar views on many of the questions facing the Reform party. Both opposed organic change and believed in the union. The Brownite Sarnia *Observer* even reported secret but unsuccessful efforts to reorganize the opposition under Sicotte and Sandfield with the *Free Press* as 'the mouthpiece.'[9] Realignment was afoot.

At this point a despondent Brown abandoned control of his own editorial desk for several months, and the *Globe* abandoned British liberalism and the union of 1841 for radical democracy and separatism. The split between Blackburn and Brown became final. The author of the *Globe*'s editorial revolution was George Sheppard, a phlegmatic journalist from England who already had behind him a brilliant career there and in the United States. In Canada, Sheppard was a close friend of the Clear Grit Charles Clarke; both men had had Chartist and other radical democratic connections. With Brown unattentive and with disapproval of Draper's decision active in the Peninsula, Sheppard's influence quickly grew at the *Globe* until by mid-May 1859 it was dominant. The *Globe* suddenly advocated the abandonment of British parliamentary government – which had turned out 'to be a cheat, a delusion, a snare'[10] – the establishment of American-style democracy, the direct election of executive officers whose powers would be exceedingly limited, and the dissolution of the union. The campaign, which was a throwback to original Clear Grittism, called into question the whole Canadian evolutionary tradition. Sandfield and Blackburn were dismayed. The daily *Free Press*, Sandfield's little weekly *Freeholder* and many other Reform journals all came out against the new *Globe* line. The *Free Press*, arguing for Sandfield, challenged Brown's entire ability to lead.[11]

If Brown did not suddenly bestir himself, Upper Canada seemed

7 *LFP*, 18 April 1859.
8 *LFP* reprint in the *Times* (Hamilton), 28 April 1859.
9 Reprinted in the *Globe*, 26 May 1859.
10 11 May 1859.
11 4, 6, 15 June and 19 July 1859.

headed for a genuine three-party division: a Conservative party led by John A. Macdonald; a liberal, reform but parliament-oriented party, inspired by the memory of Robert Baldwin, led by Sandfield Macdonald; and a separatist, American-oriented democratic party led perhaps by Sheppard. It was not to be so. After all, Brown, like Sandfield, was in the British liberal tradition. Early in the summer, he began to reassert his authority. Advocating the division of Canada into a federation, and reaffirming Canadian desire to annex the Northwest, he laid plans for a great Upper Canadian Reform convention. It opened in Toronto on 9 November 1859 with about 570 delegates, half of whom came from west of Toronto and very few east of Coburg. Although Sandfield did not attend, his brother Donald gave a keynote address condemning dissolution as totally unacceptable to the eastern, Montreal-centred counties. Blackburn, who was warned that he might be kicked down the stairs if he appeared and who like Sandfield did not approve of the convention, secured accreditation, along with several other anti-Grit delegates, but only with great difficulty.[12] The Brownite federalists were clearly in control of arrangements, although Sheppard and the radicals who demanded dissolution and democracy probably had the support of a majority of the delegates. The *Free Press*, which supported Sheppard in his opposition to expensive federalism and Brown in his opposition to destroying the economic unity of the united province, claimed that after Sheppard's principal speech he clearly could have carried the hall two to one.[13]

This would have been quite unacceptable to Sandfield and the Baldwinites. It would also have finished George Brown. At the eleventh hour, William McDougall, on Brown's behalf, introduced an amendment to Brown's key federalist resolution advocating the establishment of 'two or more local governments' charged with 'all matters of a local or sectional character.' In describing the common instrument 'charged with such matters as are necessarily common to both sections of the Province,' McDougall's amendment substituted the euphemistic phrase, 'some joint authority,' for the centralist phrase 'a general government.' The amended resolution, pushed by the federalists but with its wording apparently emphasizing division, passed almost

12 *LFP*, supplement of 18 Nov. 1859 and 19 June 1860.
13 *Ibid.*, 11 Nov. 1859.

unanimously. Then, after the convention, Brownites chose boldly to interpret 'some joint authority' as if it read 'strong federal government' and to press it on all Reformers and the assembly itself. Sheppard, who angrily left the *Globe* in January 1860, claimed that through Brown's misuse of the revised resolution, the convention had become 'a swindle.'[14] On this, Sandfield and the *Free Press* agreed. 'Some joint authority' was meaningless and 'puerile.' Federation was not the policy of the party; it was the current advocacy of a vain and failing man who had 'bambouseled' delegates at the convention. If all Upper Canadian voters were considered, the *Free Press* argued on Sandfield's behalf, Brown now represented the smallest of three Reform factions and the radical 'democratic' separatists the second largest, while the reliable old Baldwin-type group, 'the constitutional party of Reformers,' was the largest. Furthermore, it was only with this latter group that the great body of Lower Canadian Reformers could work. Representation by population remained an ultimate goal of Reformers, but until this was politically feasible so that French Canadians did not feel threatened, Sandfield's just principle of the double majority ought to prevail.[15]

Sandfield himself was determined to overthrow Brown. He would forge an Upper Canadian team of himself, Blackburn and Michael Foley. As he told an Upper Canadian Reform caucus, which in a reversal of tactics he attended on 8 March 1860, he vehemently opposed all schemes tending toward dissolution. He reaffirmed his faith in the constitutional policy of Baldwin and Lafontaine. For Lower Canadian support he looked to Sicotte. Indeed Holton had already reported to Brown increased contacts between Sicotte and restless Bleus who were worried over Cartier's economic policy and his apparent unconcern with mounting dissension in Upper Canada. The *Free Press* reported the germs of a J. Sandfield Macdonald–Sicotte alliance, antagonistic to both the Brown–Dorion and the Cartier–Macdonald régimes, 'likely to be stronger than the former and therefore more likely to supplement the latter.' Although Brown still had more parliamentary supporters than Sandfield and Foley, they were largely 'nobodies and neophytes.' Surprisingly, the Liberal Montreal *Herald* was expressing

14 Clarke Papers, Sheppard to Clarke, 27 Nov. 1859.
15 *LFP*, 24 Nov. 1859, and its weekly version the *Canadian Free Press*, 3, 10, 17 and 24 Feb. 1860.

similar views. Yet Brown had introduced and was pushing in the Assembly the resolutions of the reform convention; Sandfield's friend Thibaudeau warned seriously and darkly of the possibility of bloody warfare 'between Upper and Lower Canada.'[16] At this point Foley, who had attended the convention and spoken out eloquently against dissolution, now took Sandfield's line and enthusiastically denounced Brown's federalism. At an Upper Canadian opposition caucus which continued for four days early in the Easter recess, Sandfield and four other eastern members served notice that they would oppose his resolutions; Donald, Foley and three others refused to disclose their intentions. These ten plus two more recruits met privately in Sandfield's rooms and decided to move an amendment in the Assembly against any basic constitutional change until after an election.[17]

Sandfield then rushed back to Cornwall where, on 2 April, Christine gave birth to a son, George Sandfield Macdonald. The proud father was indeed relieved. He had had several problems at home already that year, and Christine's health had not been good. Two years earlier she had had another daughter, Cecilla Cora, who had been fragile like her first-born, and had been just hanging on to life. Although his legal practice had adjusted to the now unfavourable economic climate, it had necessitated more attention than usual just when he had been forced to intervene in the operation of the little *Freeholder*. Normally he paid little attention to this sideline; the paper existed primarily to promote his political interests and help keep the home front secure. Now he had had to find a new editor. The new man, J. E. Doyle, was swinging the paper toward a cautious approval of interest in the Northwest, which with its rich soil, he argued, should eventually form an integral part of the united province of Canada. Sandfield had also run into irritating problems with the counties council; partly to help placate moderate Conservatives in council, he eulogistically presented it with a fine portrait of Archibald McLean, his old master, the judge who had decided against Donald.

Now from Ivy Hall, with his son and Christine faring well, Sandfield, on 8 April 1860, prepared a lengthy analytical letter for Josiah Blackburn, his chief journalistic supporter. He 'scratched' the draft

16 *Canadian Free Press*, 16 March 1860.

17 Josiah Blackburn Papers in the possession of Walter J. Blackburn, London, JSM to Blackburn, 8 April 1860; a draft version exists in the JSM Papers.

so badly that he had his seventeen-year-old daughter, Lilla, copy out a final version. Admitting in a postscript that his writing at best was 'dreadfully bad,' he complained of being extremely 'nervous'; actually his penmanship was deteriorating with his health. Rejecting Blackburn's suggestion that some supporters might possibly cross the floor and join up with moderate Upper Canadian Conservatives who were not 'corruptionists,' Sandfield urged use of the term 'Baldwin Reformers' for their group. Victory would have to await an election and depended upon isolating Brown and increasing ties with Rouge, Mauve and restless Bleu. The press, he argued, must justify Upper Canadian abandonment of the convention decisions. For Sandfield, being a Baldwinite did not mean slowing down on reforms or playing the part of an old-fashioned aristocratic whig.[18] He believed that Reformers, while pressing hard for liberal administrative, fiscal and social reforms, should emphasize the integrity and duality of Canada, the cooperation of English- and French-speaking party supporters, and the maintenance of the British connection and the parliamentary system. Like Baldwin, he argued that to be viable, Reformers had to avoid doctrinaire, sectarian and sectional stands.

Back in the assembly in early May, Sandfield again presented his position in a lengthy and historically oriented speech of 'unadorned eloquence,' which the *Free Press* called 'one of the most truthful manly speeches ever delivered on the floor of the House.'[19] He defended the union and the actual and potential progress made possible by it. Unrestrained sectionalism particularly western agitation, and the wrong men in government, not the constitution, were the problems. Bleu backbenchers should be ashamed of themselves for maintaining in power a sick régime which had such little support in Upper Canada. If population trends continued in the future, he could support a move toward representation by population; meanwhile, the double majority ought to prevail. Finally, amid cheers from the treasury benches, he unequivocally endorsed the anti-Brown interpretation of the Reform entente on the seigneurial question.[20]

On 8 May Brown's resolutions finally came to a vote. Only 27 voted for declaring the union a failure, and only 32 for re-division with

18 *Ibid.*
19 *LFP*, 9 May 1860.
20 *Ibid.*, 5, 7 and 9 May 1860.

'some joint authority.' On the first count all but two voting with Brown were Upper Canadians and on the second, all but four, including McGee and Dorion. But Sandfield and Blackburn lost as much as Brown, because on both counts Foley voted with Brown. Just a few weeks earlier the *Globe* had lashed out at Foley, accusing him of disrupting the party. Foley, backed by the *Free Press*, had fought back. He had urged Reformers not to be seduced by 'the tortured misrepresentation of ill-natured and sour-minded seekers after sectional supremacy, nor by the ungenerous and malicious coloured emanations of the biddable scribblers who follow in their wake.'[21] Nevertheless, in the end, he and others had temporarily capitulated, presumably under the barrage of accusations of moral turpitude for deserting their stand at the convention. Under the circumstances, the disheartened Sandfield, as well as Donald and several other Baldwinites, absented themselves from the final vote, thereby giving Brown a technical and unreal Upper Canadian majority (25 to 22 and 28 to 27). Only three of the plotters actually voted against Brown.

With reconstruction frustrated, the personal feud between Sandfield and Brown continued in vitriolic abuse. Repeatedly throughout the spring and summer the two Reformers attacked each other in lengthy published letters which were endorsed by their respective journalistic supporters. Brown's language reached new depths of bitterness; Sandfield was more poetically sarcastic. Sandfield, who used the written testimony of Foley and a colleague of his to substantiate the position he had taken in 1859 on the seigneurial claims, referred to a protocol of Brown's which allegedly substantiated his position.[22] This was never produced, and Brown privately wrote Holton that Sandfield was a 'most unprincipled scoundrel.'[23]

Neither Baldwinites nor Grits were ready to have an election. A sudden summer rift in Upper Canadian Conservatism saved them. The Orange Lodge accused John A. Macdonald of grossly mishandling the royal visit of the Prince of Wales by not succeeding in persuading the Duke of Newcastle to have the young prince pass under arches

21 *Ibid.*, 17 April 1860.
22 *Ibid.*, 18 May, 4, 8, 10, 19 July 1860; *Gazette* (Montreal), 15 May 1860; and *Globe*, 2 June, 9 July 1860.
23 Mackenzie Papers, 3 Aug. 1860.

with Orange insignia in several towns along the shore of Lake Ontario. The election was postponed to give John A. time to mend fences. For the Reformers, the delay cost them the much needed support of organs of the Green Irish in Toronto who swung over to John A. when Brown briefly and unsuccessfully flirted with the frustrated Orange Irish. Naturally, despite Foley's conciliatory efforts, the breach between Sandfield and Brown remained.

For Sandfield and Canada the session of 1861, which opened on 16 March, seemed remarkably barren. The overtaxed Brown was severely ill and missed the entire session, while the *Globe*, dropping federalism, returned to simple representation by population. At various times Oliver Mowat, McDougall and Foley each tried to speak for the western Reformers. Sandfield stayed away from the Upper Canadian caucus, declaring at one point that he would rather see the group damned than attend; instead he preached the double majority, kept up his close personal ties with Foley, and increased his cooperation and contacts with Sicotte and other French Canadians. His heart was heavy. Cecilla Cora, his frail little daughter, had died in November. At the *Freeholder*, Doyle had proved unsatisfactory; with great difficulty Sandfield had secured the services of William Oliver, formerly of the Baldwinite *Erie News*. Progress toward political reorganization remained slow. In fact, the crafty Orange Conservative, T. R. Ferguson, by moving in March for representation by population, produced a clash between Sandfield and Foley; Sandfield called the motion inopportune and premature and dangerous to central Canada. Thibaudeau and others declared that representation by population would be resisted 'by force' if necessary. Foley retorted that talk like this could lead to an 'irrepressible conflict' such as that which seemed to be erupting south of the border. Foley, the Grits, and even Donald all voted for the unsuccessful motion.[24] But Foley swung back to Sandfield by seconding Sandfield's amendment criticizing the government for ruling without an Upper Canadian majority. The eastern Upper Canadian delegation was reunited, and the amendment was backed by Sicotte, Dorion, and Thibaudeau. The government now reluctantly declared that the basis of representation was an open question. The double majority lost by 49 votes to 62. On 19 April John A., urg-

24 *LFP*, 22 and 23 March 1861.

ing Canadians to examine the failure of American democracy and to prepare for a future centralized union of all British America in alliance with Great Britain, ridiculed the disruptive Grit position.

Suddenly Sandfield found himself physically in the middle, between the Upper Canadian proponents of the Conservative and Grit positions on the future of Canada. Earlier Cartier, who had mocked representation by population by declaring that codfish off Gaspé had as much right to representation as all the Grits of the Peninsula, had courted eastern Upper Canadians by praising their unifying role. Now John A., emphasizing the bonds tying central Canadians to Lower Canada, chastised his former junior partner, Oliver Mowat, for his leading role in the disruptive tactics of the Peninsula Grits. When Mowat retorted sharply, the Conservative chieftain literally flung himself on to the Grit. John Sandfield, the semi-invalid, the Reform spokesman of central Canada who upheld the integrity and duality of his country, forcibly pulled the combatants apart.

On the constitutional question, Sandfield was closer to his namesake than to the Grit, but on most non-sectional economic issues, Grits and Baldwinites, Rouges and Mauves could still unite. Sandfield, seconded by Dorion and backed by Sicotte, moved censure of the government for its alleged financial mismanagement. Galt's statement revealed another deficit, a growing provincial debt and increased expenditures, arising in part from unauthorized emergency advances to the Grand Trunk and other transportation interests. Speaking for Sandfield, the *Free Press* called such monopolistic favouritism much worse than socialism.[25] Debate on the censure motion, which failed by only ten votes, almost persuaded several restless Bleus to desert Premier Cartier.

Nevertheless, in the election campaign that spring both Sandfield and the Grits were at a disadvantage. Reform disunity was the greatest Conservative asset, and the government's declaration that the representational question was open enabled John Carling, the London brewer, and other Peninsula Conservatives to come out resolutely for representation by population. This partially deprived Grits of the beneficial effects of the clearly anticipated census figures which would indicate Upper Canada's population to be 1,396,091 to Lower Canada's 1,111,566.

25 *Ibid.*, 3 May 1861.

Sandfield's own position provincially within Reform was stronger than it had been in 1857. His rival Brown was physically weak and under assault from various sides; the *Free Press* called him a governmental impossibility';[26] and his stand against state aid to denominational colleges kept the powerful Wesleyan Methodist vote alienated. Foley could hardly be taken seriously as a compromise candidate for leadership. He had no support or ties in Lower Canada, was virtually rejected by the Grits, and was consuming alcohol at such a ferocious rate that he was often as drunk as the attorney general west. Although anathema to Brown and without a large personal following, Sandfield was the man with the experience and with the ties to French Canada and to mercantile Montreal. Yet in his own United Counties this 'leader of the Central Canada party' was in trouble. When his man in Stormont suddenly declined to run, Sandfield allowed his own name to stand there as well as in Cornwall. Brown and the 'Toronto junta' established a local rival to the *Freeholder* and put up Grit candidates in both ridings. Angered, Sandfield broke his customary quiet campaigning by delivering a stinging address in Cornwall on 3 July. The cry for representation by population, he charged, actually kept the 'coalition' in power and at the same time threatened the union. Disruption would be disastrous for central Canada. 'To Montreal we send our grain, our timber, our ashes. From Montreal we obtain our money.' As the Conservative Montreal *Gazette* was later to affirm, eastern Upper Canada, Montreal and the Eastern Townships were one unit. If the situation much deteriorated, he concluded, it might be advisable to transfer the area between the Ottawa and Trent rivers from Upper to Lower Canada.[27]

When the votes were counted the government had won an insecure majority in both sections. Brown went down to personal defeat. Although Donald won Glengarry by acclamation and John Sandfield held Cornwall 374 to 260, he lost Stormont to the Grits, and the Conservatives won Dundas. Sicotte and the opposition somewhat improved their position in Lower Canada, although in Montreal Cartier personally defeated Dorion, while mercantile hostility had persuaded Holton not to run at all. In Lower Canada, the growing ultramontanism of an increasingly powerful church helped shift opposition

26 *Ibid.*, 26 June 1861.
27 *Ibid.*, 4 July 1861.

against the Bleus from the radical, anti-clerical Rouges to the more moderate Mauves. Sicotte, who had endorsed the double majority, had also declared that under no circumstances would he join an administration containing George Brown. For Reformers the future seemed to lie with Sandfield and Sicotte, not Brown and Dorion.

A few weeks after the election, the battle of Bull Run brought home to Sandfield and other Canadians the bloodiness of the civil war which was now raging on their continent. For Canadians neutrality would be difficult, disinterest impossible. Growing tension between the governments of Britain and the United States raised the real possibility of warfare along the Great Lakes – St Lawrence frontier. The question of defence became critical. Argument over the degree of Canadian responsibility, particularly financial responsibility, for the defence of Canada would bring John Sandfield Macdonald to the premiership of his country. Unlike Brown, Blackburn and many other Upper Canadian Reformers, Sandfield had not been active in the anti-slavery movement; yet he did oppose the peculiar institution. General Reform sympathy for the North was, however, made difficult by Secretary of State Seward's wild talk of manifest destiny, by Lincoln's refusal to identify the Northern cause with anti-slavery, and by the belligerently annexationist line of many Northern newspapers, particularly the New York *Herald*. Sandfield's *Freeholder*, the *Free Press* and most other Baldwinite journals soon became both anti-slavery and anti-Northern. In the *Freeholder*, Oliver declared that the North, with its democratic tyranny and illiberality, had ceased to be a 'free country,' that there the 'rabble' and 'the mob' seemed sovereign and even more dangerous than the 'dictatorial powers' which Lincoln was wisely assuming.[28] For Sandfield the civil war also had a personal complication. Christine's family was of the Southern gentry, and her younger brother, Eugene, soon became a Confederate colonel.

For Canadians generally it took the imminent threat of war and Northern invasion to silence temporarily the endemic bickering. Bloodshed seemed almost inevitable when in November a Yankee captain forcibly removed Confederate agents from the British steamer *Trent*. Men from the sedentary militia rushed to the colours; English Canada, like French Canada, was concerned with *la survivance*. Ulti-

28 JSM Papers, *Freeholder*, 26 Aug. 1861.

mately, sober heads in London and Washington prevailed. Tension continued into 1862, but the immediate danger of massive fighting on Canadian soil lessened.

As the decisive Americans continued to butcher one another, Sandfield and the other frock-coated Victorian gentlemen who spoke for the Canadians returned to what they were helping to make a chief characteristic of their half-born nation, to interminable discussion over the nature, responsibility and destiny of their cherished but strange country. Sandfield was there when the new parliament met on 20 March, to engage in arguments over defence as well as over the old issues. As usual he found the opposition divided, but his own position steadily improved. After the caucus of western Reformers picked Foley over Mowat as house leader, Sandfield ended his boycott of its meetings. He was pleased when Sicotte not only became the Lower Canadian chieftain but also the titular leader of the opposition. Then when McDougall secured Foley's reluctant backing for the standard resolution favouring representation by population, Sandfield combined with Sicotte, and Cartier too, to defeat the measure. As Sandfield's prestige in French Canada rose, he worked with Sicotte, who claimed that the union was a compact between English and French, on a bill to solve the Grand Trunk financial dilemma by unifying that line with the Great Western and by changing most bondholders into stockholders. With the government favouring the measure, Grits were convinced that it was another trick to rob the taxpayers. As the voice of Toronto liberal business interests, the *Globe* was also disturbed by the bill's lack of dedication to the sacredness of private property. Such a lapse did not trouble Sandfield. As one might expect, his concern was pragmatically with the social need to save the line. When in the face of scandal over contracts, the government stopped work on the Parliament Buildings in Ottawa, it was Sandfield who secured the establishment of an investigating committee. Richard Scott, a Catholic Conservative from Ottawa, introduced a bill to expand the rights of Upper Canadian Catholic schools, and the Grits were as loud in their denunciation as McGee was in his praise. The two Sandfields took a middle line: personally against separate schools and opposed to them in Glengarry, they favoured the 'right' of the minority to such schools.

Suddenly both the railway bill and the school bill were thrust aside by the crisis over Cartier's militia bill.[29] Cartier's proposed legislation provided for the implementation of a portion of a royal commission report on defence. The report urged a reorganization of the militia which alone would cost over a million dollars a year. Accepting its principles, the bill envisioned an initial defence expenditure of about $800,000 of which about half would be spent on the maintenance of a 'regular militia' of 30,000 men who would drill for four days a year. The present active or 'volunteer' militia then contained 14,000 men, only 5,000 of whom were paid. The new regular militia would be organized on a quota basis for each locality, and in rural areas where the voluntary method failed to raise the quota, conscription or the draft would prevail. Even in 1860, the last year before the war, Britain was paying the equivalent of the proposed $800,000 for the defence of Canada and was maintaining about 2,200 troops in Canada and another 2,000 in Nova Scotia. In 1861 Britain dispatched 14,000 troops to British North America, most of them going to Canada. In March 1862 the House of Commons, containing many Little Englanders and other champions of retrenchment, passed a resolution reaffirming the doctrine that self-defence was a primary corollary of internal self-government, although admitting that Britain would aid any colony attacked because of imperial policy. This resolution, which merely stated more articulately what for several years had been British intent, shocked and enraged Canadians, particularly Reformers be they Baldwinites,[30] Mauves, Rouges or Grits. The Canadian government was already running with a severe annual deficit. If war came, Canadians were loyally ready to die to help defend themselves, their country and the Empire. But the quarrel with the Americans arose primarily over imperial issues, and Canadians were not going to bankrupt the country to establish in peacetime an extravagant militia which would still be helpless without the British if the Yankees did attack.

In the Assembly Sicotte led the asault. Sandfield supported him but played no major role in the debate. His organ the *Free Press* took the responsible line that Canada should expand its defence expenditure

29 See C. P. Stacey, *Canada and the British Army* (Toronto 1963), pp. 117–23, and G. F. G. Stanley, *Canada's Soldiers, 1604–1954* (Toronto 1954), pp. 213–20.

30 *LFP*, 20 March 1862.

only up to the safe limits of its financial capacity.[31] Sicotte's strong line proved effective. On 20 May the opposition defeated the government 61 to 54.[32] In this crucial vote, 16 Lower Canadians abandoned Premier Cartier for Louis Sicotte. For eight years the Upper Canadian Reformers had tried to overthrow the government; now when the overthrow came, the government actually secured an Upper Canadian majority but lost its hold on Lower Canada. With Brown out of the Assembly and with Sicotte, not the radical Dorion, as the Lower Canadian Reform leader, it was easier for French Canadians to desert the increasingly unacceptable Cartier, the corporation lawyer for the Grand Trunk.

Whom would Governor General Monck ask to form a government? Sicotte, Foley and Sandfield were all possibilities. But Sicotte was linked both in Canada and in Britain with the defeat of the militia bill. Monck would be in serious trouble at home for his failure to secure more Canadian support of self-defence; he could hardly reward the chief architect of his disgrace. Foley had no standing outside the Western Peninsula and not a great deal within; besides, Foley's ferocious drinking reminded Monck of his outgoing minister of militia, John A. Macdonald, who had been incapacitated for much of the crucial debate. Sandfield Macdonald, though he lacked a large personal following and was disliked by the Grits, had strong ties both east and west, both French and English, and was the champion of both central Canada and the continued integrity and unity of the province. Although an opponent of Cartier's bill, he had not played a major role in its defeat. Therefore, on Victoria's birthday, 1862, John Sandfield Macdonald, the only logical choice, became attorney general west, minister of militia affairs and premier of Canada. The long quest had ended. Yet how could the broken ranks of Reform ever hope to govern a Canada beset by the growing centrifugal forces within it?

31 *Ibid.*, 3, 9, 20 March, 16 April, 14, 15, 16 May 1862.
32 *Ibid.*, 21 May 1862, and *JLA*, 1862, pp. 228–29.

4

The Premier from Cornwall

As premier, John Sandfield Macdonald devoted himself almost exclusively to his political and administrative responsibilities. He tried resolutely to create a Reform alliance which might sustain power, proceed with the long-awaited reforms, and counteract sectional, sectarian and ethnic tensions tearing apart the society and body politic of the province. Sandfield also had to cope with the hostility with which Canada and his government were viewed in Britain, to work out an acceptable militia policy, and to establish good relations with his ruffled governor general. He had parliament wind up its routine business and then not reassemble for almost nine months. During most of this time Christine remained with her children at Ivy Hall; indeed Sandfield may have been home only three times: once to secure his reelection, once on a tour with the governor general when he stayed for part of the local assizes, and finally for the Christmas holiday season. As usual, when he was in Cornwall, Ivy Hall echoed to the sounds of laughter, bagpipes, trilingual chatter, and the popping of corks from champagne bottles. His moments of family and community life were rare and short.

He began his premiership in good spirits, by seeing to it that control of the government was predominantly in the hands of the Baldwinites and Mauves. Sicotte was the Lower Canadian Leader and attorney general east; Dorion, who lacked an Assembly seat and was the only Rouge in the cabinet, was merely provincial secretary. McGee was President of Council. The Upper Canadian portion had three moderates, including the premier and Foley, and three Grits. McDougall, the Grit lieutenant accepted the temptation of office and brought his friend William Howland to the finance portfolio. The *Globe*, whose publisher had himself changed his mind twice in recent years as to the solution for the constitutional dilemma, bitterly denounced McDougall and the other two Grits for abandonment of principle; it was 'enough to sicken a horse.'[1] McDougall never again regained the confidence of George Brown, who described the Upper Canadian ministers as a 'set of Jackasses,'[2] and more and more came to rely on Oliver Mowat and Alexander Mackenzie. Sandfield was hereby inadvertently preparing the way for the future Grit premier of Ontario and the future Grit prime minister of Canada. Recognizing 'the Federal character' of the union, the government pledged itself to see that the full cabinet dealt with most matters common to both sections; the portion from each section was primarily responsible for its sectional affairs. Each half of the administration, it was agreed, 'should possess the confidence of a majority of its representatives,' and local legislation should not be carried against the wishes of a sectional majority. The government would expand the active militia using the 'volunteer movement' and ease the burden on creditors. It would establish representation by population within a section, hold to Ottawa as the future capital, thoroughly investigate the situation concerning the Parliament Buildings, and finally, secure financial and administrative reorganization, rigid retrenchment and a balanced budget.[3]

The London *Free Press* gave Sandfield's régime its total blessing, and a great many Reform journals, including the Montreal *Herald*, followed suit. Leading Conservative papers treated the government gingerly but bitterly attacked the *Globe* for its alleged negative attitude.[4] Still the premier needed more secure journalistic support in Quebec City, which remained the temporary capital. At first the Quebec *Chronicle* had been quite friendly, but its owner was also proprietor of the *Prototype*, rival of the *Free Press* in London. Sandfield therefore tried to work through the independent and rather inconsequential tri-weekly *Mercury*. In the autumn of 1862 the erratic, ubiquitous but

1 *Globe*, 27 May 1862.
2 Mackenzie Papers, Brown to Holton, 29 May 1862.
3 *LFP*, 28 May 1862.
4 *Ibid.*, 29, 30, 31 May 1862.

now more temperate George Sheppard moved from the *Chronicle* to the *Mercury*, improving the latter's quality and increasing its identification with the government. By 2 December 1862 Sandfield himself had secretly leased the *Mercury* and persuaded Blackburn to come down to the seat of government as publisher; Sheppard remained editor. Within six weeks the *Mercury* became, despite the bitter derision of the *Chronicle*, an effective daily with qualified political reporters. With a small English-language market, the *Mercury* could only be sustained at a great financial loss, which was partly eased by obtaining from the government a 'large quantity' of printing contracts. Although this piece of patronage was usual practice, it proved controversial in the light of rumours of Sandfield's personal involvement.[5] Certainly he made no money on the venture, and a supporting organ in the capital was essential.

Meanwhile, Sandfield set about initiating his program. He persuaded Richard Scott to postpone his separate school bill. Before prorogation on 9 June 1862, he secured approval of an interim measure, doubling the size of the paid voluntary militia to 10,000 soldiers, and further promoting service in unpaid units, all at a cost not to exceed $250,000. This was a sum three times that spent in 1861; Monck was thankful but far from satisfied. Sandfield agreed to abandon the fusion of the Grand Trunk and Great Western railways. But with the approbation of C. J. Brydges, general manager of the Grand Trunk, and E. W. Watkin, the railway's special agent from England, as well as the Colonial Office, Sandfield secured the passage of a measure providing for changing many bondholders into stockholders, reducing the remaining interest rates, and futher adjusting fiscal arrangements. He also persuaded the legislature to accept past expenditures on the controversial Parliament Buildings where work remained arrested, and after prorogation he had a royal commission appointed to investigate the scandals. Finally, he had Monck appoint a commission, which included George Sheppard, to report on fiscal and departmental reorganizations.

Although Monck seemed partially prepared to accept Sandfield's action and promises on imperial relations, Newcastle remained sceptical and annoyed. Goaded by the anti-Canadian line of the *Times*,

5 *Quebec Mercury* (henceforth *QM*), 20 and 29 Nov. and 2 Dec. 1864, and *LFP*, 21 March 1864.

the small but influential Little England lobby was giving the Colonial and War Offices a hard time. Newcastle had nothing but disdain for the double majority, the expansion of the volunteer militia and the ministry in general.[6] In August, Monck, the man in the middle, lost patience and informed his secretary of state that, while he had no doubts whatsoever on the score of loyalty, he did not have 'a very high opinion of Mr J. S. Macdonald's abilities' or of his firmness of purpose. Monck, like Elgin, Head and other governors general, was at times inclined to see Canadian partisanship as petty, in contrast with what seemed to them great issues of state dividing public men at home. The Reform ministers were a 'wretched lot,' none of them 'capable of rising above the level of a parish politician.'[7] Sandfield would never see this letter. It would have mitigated against the close and lasting friendship which was soon to develop between the two men. On 21 August, Newcastle sent Monck and the cabinet an official statement on defence which virtually demanded a trained active militia of about 50,000 men and bluntly asserted that the defence of Canada was primarily a Canadian responsibility.[8] Newcastle and Sandfield could not know how different would be the situation seventy-eight years later when it was Britain that stood singularly exposed and Canada which answered the call for help. For the moment Sandfield was in a tight corner.

Neither his government, nor perhaps any Canadian régime, could survive an attempt to fulfill Newcastle's demands. But perhaps the premier could extricate himself by means of the related Intercolonial railway from the terminus of the Grand Trunk at Rivière du Loup to Halifax. Urged on by Watkin, who was becoming quite the friend of the premier, the British now seemed prepared, on grounds of defence, to guarantee a loan of £3,000,000 if the line kept well back from the American border. With Joseph Howe and Leonard Tilley representing the Maritimes and with Sandfield as lavish Canadian host, an interprovincial conference of ministers at Quebec in September 1862 agreed to seek British backing, share the costs, and construct the line. For Sandfield the political price was high. He, T. D'Arcy McGee, and

6 PAC, Newcastle Papers (on microfilm), Newcastle to Monck, 6 and 14 June and 26 July 1862, and JSM Papers, E. Watkin to JSM, 26 June 1862.
7 Newcastle Papers, 11 Aug. 1862.
8 *Globe*, 16 March 1863.

the Montreal business community were enthusiastic about the railway, but within two days of the agreement Dorion ceased attending cabinet. The Rouges were unalterably opposed to such costly and corruption-encouraging ventures, which seemed unrelated to French-Canadian progress, liberalism and democracy and which tended in the direction of union with the Maritimes. The line was also not popular with Grits, because of its cost and the involvement with hated Grand Trunk interests; for them the west, where the ineffectual rule of the Hudson's Bay Company had to be eliminated, not the east, had priority. McGee learned from Holton, who had a letter from Brown in Britain, that all but W. E. Gladstone in the British government were determined to see a railway built from the Atlantic to the Pacific.[9] The cabinet arranged for Sicotte and Howland to go overseas to join Maritime delegates in negotiations with the British government. On McGee's urging the Canadians were told to secure the best possible terms from Britain. The premier wanted the Canadian contribution to the line recognized as a major commitment to imperial defence, and he intended to reject Newcastle's demands for the large volunteer force. Yet this was still too much for Dorion, who publicly submitted his resignation, and too little for Monck who firmly requested a large active militia, preferably secured by the ballot or the draft.

On 24 October the cabinet, in a formal minute of council, forthrightly answered both Monck and Newcastle. Respectfully and loyally worded, the minute was Sandfield's most important state paper. Rejecting Newcastle's demands and his colonial theory, it set out a position which clearly previewed the future stand of such Liberals as Sir Wilfrid Laurier. A costly Canadian military establishment, the brief stated, could only be justified in periods of 'imminent danger or actual war'; Canadians had no severe quarrel with the Americans and would have no knowledge of nor any role in a rupture of British relations with Washington. 'So dire a calamity' as war, which 'would be disastrous' to every Canadian interest, would not proceed from any Canadian action. Yet if war came, Canada would fully do her duty. The expenditure requested by Newcastle could be obtained only by direct taxation, and any attempt to obtain it in peacetime would destroy a

9 JSM Papers, McGee to JSM, 2 Oct. 1862, and Mackenzie Papers, Brown to Holton, 3 Sept. 1862.

Canadian government. To borrow would, at the moment, endanger Canadian credit with 'European capitalists.' Nevertheless, the volunteer force would be expanded. Finally, Newcastle's suggestion that funds for the army be placed beyond the annual supervision of the legislature was intolerable and 'ought not to be entertained by a people inheriting the freedom guaranteed by British institutions.'[10] Here was the Baldwinite Sandfield at his liberal best; on this aspect of responsible government, he later declared that his cabinet had answered Newcastle's impertinences 'in fitting terms becoming a people enjoying British freedom.'[11] Gradually Sandfield brought Monck around to the realization that a progressive expansion of the volunteer force was, at least politically, the best that could be expected. But in England, Sicotte and Howland were coolly received. Gladstone demanded that the colonies set up a sinking fund to cover the required imperial guarantee of bonds for the railway. Although Gladstone temporized somewhat, Sicotte remained disturbed and uncommitted. The Canadians did not sign. Newcastle told Monck that he had 'utterly' rejected the 'monstrous proposal' that Sandfield's government could regard spending on the Intercolonial as spending on defence; furthermore he regarded the cabinet's brief as 'bunkum.'[12] It apparently never occurred to His Grace that he was denying to Sandfield the very argument that he and his colleagues planned to use to sell the railway to the British parliament. What was sauce for Newcastle's imperial goose was apparently not to be used as sauce for Sandfield's colonial gander.

In January Sandfield told Premier Tilley, who was then in Quebec, that while the Intercolonial was not abandoned, Canada could at the moment, in the light of Gladstone's and Newcastle's stand and their refusal to help in any way with opening the 'Western Country,' only participate in a joint survey for the route. Politically, Sandfield could hardly extend himself for the Intercolonial if nothing was to be forthcoming about the west. Emphasizing the political and financial difficulties, Sandfield assured Tilley of his sincere dedication to the Intercolonial and of his willingness to resign if he thought it would help

10 *Globe*, 16 March 1863.

11 Canada, *Parliamentary Debates on the Subject of the Confederation of the British North American Provinces* (henceforth *Conf. Debates*) (Quebec 1865), p. 724.

12 Newcastle Papers, 20 Nov. 1862.

matters.[13] The *Globe* cheered when the government publicly announced a delay in construction.[14]

So busy had Sandfield been with these and other matters that he had been able to spend only a few days around the Christmas season with Christine at Ivy Hall. Even there the Civil War intruded itself. He shared his wife's anxiety for the safety of her Southern relatives, and helped where he could. At the battle of Malvern Hill, Federal troops captured her brother, Colonel Eugene Waggaman, and imprisoned him near Boston. Through banking friends of Christine's in New York, Sandfield supplied his brother-in-law with certain comforts. Having already established a relationship with Secretary of State Seward, the Canadian premier negotiated personally for Eugene's release and for his confinement in Canada under his own charge for the duration of the war. Eugene, however, declined the offer and later benefitted from a prisoner exchange. He continued fighting until he surrendered the remnant of the Second Louisiana Brigade with Robert E. Lee at Appomattox. Meanwhile, Sandfield maintained his Northern contacts, writing occasionally to Seward and also to Charles Sumner. In fact he had to cancel at the last minute a projected visit to Sumner in Washington during January 1863. Urgent 'matters of state,' he gave as the reason;[15] the imminent meeting of a troublesome parliament was the cause.

When parliament did open, it was with more formality and martial pomp than usual, and the morale of the premier and government was high and still rising. In both sections of the country, the *Mercury* argued, the strength of the ministry was growing daily. For the moment the double majority was not a 'humbug' or an 'abstract' theory, but a vital preservative practice.[16] Liberals, said the *Free Press*, had gained only as they turned from Brown to Sandfield, a man who stood 'between the extremes of party,' moderate yet a constant reformer, a man on whom 'no stain ever sullied his reputation.'[17] Helping to placate the Grits, Sandfield had Foley announce on 9 February that tenders were now invited to initiate postal service from

13 *Ibid.*, Tilley to Arthur Gordon, 2 Feb. 1863.
14 6 and 19 Jan. 1863.
15 University of Rochester, Rush Rees Library, William Henry Seward Collection, JSM to Seward, 31 Dec. 1863.
16 3 and 5 Feb. 1863.
17 13 Jan. 1863.

Fort William to Red River. Helping to placate the British and conservatively oriented Canadians, Sandfield could announce that the volunteer force now exceeded 25,000 men. The speech from the throne proudly reviewed the record and the progress of the royal commissions, talked of further communication links with colonies as far away as British Columbia, and announced plans for intra-sectional representation by population.

Sandfield's optimism was ill founded. All of the sectional, ethnic and sectarian issues which severely divided Canadians remained. Backbench Grits and fiery Orangemen continued to push for genuine representation by population, to the great embarrassment of McDougall and Howland. On 27 February 1863 R. W. Scott's innocent-looking Separate School Bill for Upper Canada, a private measure backed by members of cabinet, secured first reading. Just over three weeks earlier, on 5 January, the *Globe*, in an editorial written by George Brown's brother Gordon, had passionately attacked the 'wily' Catholic hierarchy as the enemy of progress and education, and warned Reformers against any concession whatsoever to the 'enemy' on the school system. But neither Sandfield, Ryerson, nor McDougall seemed perturbed; the bill hardly involved any new principle, and the three men expected more trouble from a grammar school measure which lacked sectarian overtones. Basically, the Scott bill merely tidied up and clarified the vague wording of the Taché Act of 1855 and consolidated that act and earlier statutes. It did, however, remove the necessity for an annual declaration by separate school supporters and the requirement that separate school rates be at least as high as public rates. It also gave separate school trustees the right to license teachers. Originally the bill had gone much further toward two parallel systems, but during the previous June, Ryerson, with Sandfield's approval, had not only had the bill severely watered down but had secured from both Scott and representatives of the Catholic hierarchy a commitment, which he communicated to the press, that the bill would be 'accepted' as a final settlement. At that time the premier had told the chief superintendent how happy he was that his government could now settle so easily this old, vexatious problem.[18]

18 C. B. Sissons, *Egerton Ryerson: His Life and Letters* (Toronto 1947), II, 470–71, Ryerson-Hodgins Papers, Ryerson to J. G. Hodgins [3 June 1862].

On 5 March, after a stormy debate in which the Orange and Grit cores offered resolute opposition, the bill passed second reading with a double majority. That same day George Brown secured election for the riding of South Oxford which Sandfield had injudiciously opened to him by appointing Dr Connor to the bench. Brown, who had just returned at Christmas from Britain where he had been happily married to Anne Nelson, began editorializing against those Upper Canadians who had heeded Sandfield's call and voted for the bill. Brown even threatened to 'abandon politics altogether.' The *Globe* and Sandfield's *Mercury* thereupon engaged in an impassioned debate on the nature of liberals and bigots. They argued over which label applied to those who insisted on non-sectarian and non-segregated schools and which to those who compromised in the face of deep feelings of conscience on the part of a large minority who placed religion at the centre of education.[19] The premier, his brother and McDougall thereupon persuaded Scott to delete one of the few clauses that Brown could attack substantively, that giving separate school trustees the right to license teachers. Nevertheless, on 13 March, at final division, pressure from the *Globe* and local constituents this time cheated Scott and indirectly Sandfield of an Upper Canadian majority. The bill passed 74 to 30. On second reading the Upper Canadian vote had been 34 to 21 in favour; now it was 23 to 30 against. Apart from the ministers, only two Reformers voted with Sandfield Macdonald and John A. Macdonald. Even Donald found it advisable to be absent for the vote. Enraged by the Grits, Sandfield left the chamber 'in great indignation.'[20]

Sandfield later argued his case before a caucus of Upper Canadian Reformers from both houses. He wanted the bill insignificantly amended in the upper chamber and returned to the lower chamber where it would be passed by a double majority. He told Ryerson that if the Grits did not capitulate he would 'play them a game that they little anticipated.'[21] Rumours of plans to negotiate with Conservatives abounded. Although a distinct majority attending apparently capitulated to Sandfield, the Conservatives later frustrated his plans in the

19 *Globe*, 6, 10, 11 March 1863.
20 *Ibid.*, 16 March 1863.
21 Sissons, *Ryerson*, II, 481, Ryerson to Hodgins, 16 March 1863, and *LFP*, 17 March 1863.

Council, and the bill became law on 5 May. While the *Globe* condemned Sandfield for his veiled threats and Ryerson for being a 'traitor,' Brown himself was participating in secret but fruitless negotiations, with Malcolm Cameron as intermediary, towards some alliance with the Conservatives. This did not help Sandfield, whose hand was further weakened when the *Canadian Freeman*, the Irish Catholic oracle in Toronto, denied McGee's assertion concerning the finality of Scott's bill and demanded, sooner or later, 'the whole debt.' Neither Bishop Lynch's public disavowal of the editorial nor his private letter of congratulation, followed by one from Kingston's Bishop Horan, to Scott for settling 'finally our school difficulty' could correct the impression.[22] Grit- and Orange-inspired public meetings against the bill spread throughout Upper Canada.

Was the double majority dead? Was Sandfield's premiership doomed? Was it in fact true, as so many Conservatives had long maintained, that Reformers could not govern? Faced with sectarian and sectional issues could Canadian Liberals not display enough tolerant liberalism to save their government for the broad reforms on which there seemed to be general agreement? The *Free Press*, temporarily edited by Josiah Blackburn's brother Stephen, was not sure. Pretending to wonder what had happened since the session of 1862, Sandfield's *Mercury* implied that without Brown's interjection the bill would have received the double majority; it proposed nothing more than what Brown as premier had been prepared to accept in August 1858.[23] John A. now appeared to have been correct when he argued before third reading that there was a 'whip' which drove members from the government and that the whip 'was stronger than the Government.'[24]

Yet on 22 April, on a minor point, the régime was sustained, with poor attendance, by a double majority. The vital aspect of Sandfield's view of the double majority precariously survived; the government was being sustained by majorities from both sections, even though a private bill backed by cabinet had secured only a simple majority. On 22 April only 9 of the 15 Lower Canadian rebels who had moved

22 *Canadian Freeman* (Toronto), reprinted with comments in the *Globe*, 20, 21 March 1863. PAC, R. W. Scott Papers, Lynch to Scott, 18 March 1863, and telegram 6 May 1863; Horan to Scott, 24 April 1863.
23 *QM*, 16 March 1863.
24 *Globe*, 14 March 1863.

from Cartier to Sicotte in May 1862 were present; six voted with Sicotte, three were back with Cartier. Developing a close personal relationship with a buoyant Ryerson, Sandfield slowly regained some of his confidence, just when Sicotte's hold over the motley Mauves was becoming increasingly precarious. Brown was now in the house, sitting with Dorion and giving support to the régime on non-sectarian issues. As McGee declared privately, Brown's mere presence in the House was enough to send more of the Mauve-tinted chicks scurrying back to Cartier, their mother hen.[25]

With a taunting speech on 1 May 1863 John A. Macdonald moved non-confidence in the government. Sandfield replied with a speech which, Ryerson considered, was much better than usual, arguing that his opponent was all negative in his criticism and was an anomaly as a leader because a vast majority of his followers disagreed with him on vital matters affecting their section. The premier emphatically denied that the double majority was invalidated by the Scott bill. Although, despite retrenchment, Howland's budget for 1863 had forecast a deficit of three quarters of a million dollars, Sandfield's record had much to commend it. The previous deficit had been two and three quarter million dollars. The new militia bill, whose principles had already been debated, awaited second reading. Meanwhile, the volunteer force continued to grow, and Britain had now agreed to supply 25,000 rifles. McGee's bill for civil service reform had passed second reading. The report of the royal commission on the Parliament Buildings had implicated the past government in scandal and had led to new contracts at lower prices with the old contractors and to the recommencement of construction. Although both sides seemed optimistic about the vote on John A.'s motion, Ryerson was incredulous at Joseph Cauchon's claim that the opposition would secure 37 of the 64 Lower Canadian votes; but the silent Mauves were the men to watch.[26] Outside the cabinet, Rouge and Grit, Dorion, Mackenzie, Mowat, and finally Brown, all urged support for Sandfield. Brown's speech, however, frightened more than assuaged the Mauves. He reaffirmed his distaste for the present régime, but, he argued, he preferred these ministers to the old gang.

25 E. H. Cameron, *Memoirs of Ralph Vansittart* (Toronto 1924), pp. 116–17.
26 Sissons, *Ryerson*, II, 486, Ryerson to Hodgins, 2 May 1863; *QM*, 2 May 1863; *LFP*, 4 May 1863.

'He would kill them off when he could get better.'[27] What would seem better for Brown would seem *plus mauvais pour les mauves.*

The vote was taken early on the morning of 8 May. The government lost 59 to 64, but it won in Upper Canada 31 to 28, losing in Lower Canada 28 to 36. Only six of the sixteen Lower Canadian converts of 1862 remained with Sicotte. It was Dorion and the Rouges who held. Cartier obtained only one less vote than Cauchon prophesied. The premier saw Monck who quietly agreed to an imminent dissolution.

On the same weekend Sandfield, using his brother as an intermediary, negotiated with Brown, Dorion, Holton and Mowat about a possible reconstruction. The talks were long, difficult, tedious and involved. Sandfield avoided total capitulation to the Grit and Rouge groups by making use of the inherent divisions among them and by threatening to deal with the official enemy. For instance, when Brown demanded acceptance of representation by population, Dorion and Holton replied that declaring the matter an open question – as the Conservatives had done in 1861 – was as far as they could go. 'There now, did I not tell you so!' interjected Sandfield.[28] Brown and Mowat admitted bitter disappointment, but Sandfield's threats, backed this time by Dorion, ultimately forced acceptance. Nevertheless, the premier had to give up the double majority as the fundamental principle of government, although of course he could hold to it personally as the most desirable way of solving the present problem. He also had to give Dorion *carte blanche* in Lower Canada. The Intercolonial was, apparently, to be dropped. Dorion and the premier further agreed that McGee, who had antagonized many French Canadians and probably the premier himself, would have to go in favour of old L. T. Drummond. The secret talks with Brown placed Sandfield in an impossible position with several of his current ministers. During the consultations Sicotte, who resented Dorion's sudden return to eminence, resisted change and finally refused to serve under the Rouge chief despite the latter's pleading. In the end, five moderate Reformers, including Sicotte, McGee, and Foley, were out. Howland gave up finance in favour of the lesser position of receiver general; Dorion became attorney general east. Holton brought the government

27 *Globe,* 7 May 1863.
28 Brown Papers, George Brown to Gordon Brown, 11 May 1863.

great strength as minister of finance. Mowat became postmaster general. The *Mercury* regretted the absence of Sicotte and hoped that he, Foley, and McGee would remain loyal and work for the government in the election, but the *Globe* rejoiced over the composition of the government and that representation by population would be an open question.[29]

It could hardly have been a time of rejoicing for John Sandfield Macdonald. He had won his battle for survival as premier. His administrative, financial and militia reforms could still be achieved. But the government was so much less his than it had been. The moderate Reform group was disappearing. Sicotte, McGee, Foley and others were all angry. They were to seek re-election as inimical independents and then accuse Sandfield of misrepresenting their positions in the negotiations.

In the election which followed, Sandfield concentrated his efforts in eastern Upper Canada, and in areas such as London, Napanee and Hamilton where he had considerable influence. He was particularly effective against the Conservatives in the Ottawa valley, where, ironically, R. W. Scott had been building up a threatening political machine. To avoid trouble in Orange areas, John A. Macdonald did not rush in to help the Catholic. Scott and his followers were defeated. But then, after accepting the premier's aid, many of the victorious representatives, true to the 'loose fish' tradition of the valley, refused to remain loyal and were won over by John A. before parliament met – probably by utilizing the old capital question. This loss in the Ottawa valley later proved disastrous. Still the victory of Brown and Sandfield in Upper Canada resembled a rout; Reformers won between 41 and 45 seats, although Sandfield's Baldwinites emerged weaker and Brown's Grits stronger than before. The Conservatives went down in terrible defeat. John A. Macdonald entered the last parliament of the Province of Canada, the one that was to make his name immortal, with only a remnant of supporters.

For Sandfield, victory in Upper Canada was not enough, and Dorion and Holton, though they did surprisingly well, could not expect to win a majority, even though Dorion vowed to oppose both representation by population and the old agreement for the Inter-

29 *QM*, 18 and 20 May 1863, and *Globe*, 14 May 1863.

colonial. Sandfield had won a shaky single majority but not his double majority. In the vote of confidence in the previous parliament Sandfield had secured 28 Lower Canadian votes, but he had immediately lost the support of the four Lower Canadian ministers, whom he dropped, and one of their followers. In the new Assembly he would have about 25 Lower Canadian seats, that is, two more than just before the election, including only two of the converts of 1862. In Lower Canada Sandfield actually lost six seats and gained eight. In the light of Brown's increased influence, this was quite a remarkable performance. But despite the contrary claims of the *Mercury*, Sandfield could no longer govern in the image of Robert Baldwin; Dorion could never be a Lafontaine. Sandfield was not at the head of a great, truly united, bilingual and bisectional Reform party which subordinated personalities and regional and sectarian differences in favour of moderate reform and economic progress.

Nevertheless, though appearing 'crotchety' at times,[30] Sandfield fought on. Before the eighth parliament opened on 13 August he had raised the prestige of his government considerably. The Conservative press, which had previously shown him some deference, now condemned his régime forthrightly, accusing it of 'democratic and revolutionary tendencies,' but the Reform press was united in its general support. Despite pressure from Toronto, including threats of resignation from Mowat, Sandfield held firm on moving the government to Ottawa as soon as possible. He and Holton received sympathetically the report of the commission on financial and departmental reorganization that condemned the inadequate legislative supervision of public spending. Although Newcastle, always sceptical of Sandfield's intentions, informed Monck of his dissatisfaction with the reconstruction procedure and the composition of the cabinet, Monck was becoming quite attached to his first minister; he assured Newcastle of Sandfield's dependability, suggesting that Cartier's opposition was 'factious.'[31] Concerning the Intercolonial, Sandfield persuaded Dorion to agree to an outlay of $10,000 toward a survey to be undertaken by Sandford Fleming. 'I declare to God,' he told Tilley when he and

30 Sissons, *Ryerson*, II, 489, Ryerson to Hodgins, 2 July 1863.
31 Newcastle Papers, Newcastle to Monck, 20 June 1863 and Monck to Newcastle, 8 July 1863.

Tupper came to Quebec in August, 'if I thought by resigning my office we could get the Intercolonial Railway I would do it.'[32] Even concerning the Northwest, Sandfield seemed to be moving, and his ally was Edward Watkin whose growing friendship with the premier disturbed Brown. After unsuccessfully fighting the Hudson's Bay fur empire, the Grand Trunk tycoon helped buy out the old company and incline it favourably toward land development. Over the objections of the Colonial Office, Watkin and Sandfield were approaching an accord whereby Canada would financially assist the company with various colonization and communication schemes. Newcastle was openly admitting to Monck that he proposed using Canada's desire to acquire territory in the Northwest as blackmail to force Canada to spend more on defence and the Intercolonial. Sandfield had little room to manoeuvre.

The government planned to have no regular legislative session until the spring of 1864; a short meeting in August would merely handle supply and the militia bills. But the opposition kept this special session going until 15 October, trying repeatedly to win the handful of votes necessary to topple the premier. The tactics of obstruction and wrangling actually strengthened Sandfield and weakened Cartier. At one point it even looked as if Cartier would be forced to retire in favour of the still ambitious Sicotte. On 5 September, Sandfield suddenly, to the anger of the Opposition, successfully offered Sicotte a lucrative judgeship; it was rumoured that that very day a meeting of the Bleus and disgruntled ex-Mauves actually chose Sicotte as leader over Cartier. If true, Sandfield by a few hours wrested Sicotte from a rendezvous with history.

The Government's two militia bills[33] passed 74 to 25 and 75 to 21, even though they were, as Sandfield claimed, much more costly than Cartier's unsuccessful bill of 1862. All the opponents were Lower Canadians, and only two were Rouges. Cartier, who voted for the bills, had anything but a firm hold on his alleged followers. Six of the seven rebels of 1862 who had returned to Cartier and secured re-election voted negatively. The first bill set up 'service battalions' of 750 men who would receive up to six days training, to be drawn by

32 *Conf. Debates*, p. 653.
33 Canada, 27 Victoria, cap. 2 and 3.

lot from those eligible. It also provided for skilled, paid instructors and two military schools. The second bill concerned the volunteer force which would now have a limit of 35,000 men, all clothed and equipped but not paid. The defence budget for 1863 was estimated at $613,500. Despite opposition derision, the brilliant and dedicated Holton submitted for legislative approval an honest statement of all expenditures since parliament had prorogued. His report indicated an outlay in 1863 of just over $15,000,000 which necessitated a deficit of $1,500,000. Although retrenchment was clearly shown, fixed charges and new defence spending prevented a balanced budget and necessitated new taxation. A new tax bill, which would not raise tariffs, was to be introduced during the regular session. Although intemperately and unfairly ridiculed by Galt, Holton's budget and also the militia bills secured for Sandfield unusual praise in the British press; even the *Times* was ecstatic.[34]

Perhaps the most auspicious sign for Sandfield was the increasing mellowness which his arch-foe, George Brown, showed him. Sandfield and Christine, who had gone down to Quebec with the girls for the session, had rented quarters where they entertained in their usual bounteous fashion. There, in late September 1863, George Brown actually attended 'a quiet little family party of eight' where various persons played the piano or took 'a turn on the fiddle.'[35] For the moment the hateful exchanges of the past were set aside. In supporting calm serious study of the constitutional dilemma, Brown had even urged in the Assembly that the government should undertake 'the strongest efforts' to secure 'a majority in Lower Canada as well as in Upper Canada.'[36] If no one rocked the boat, there was just the outside chance that Sandfield's drive for broad reform and honest government might succeed.

Before parliament reassembled on 19 February 1864 the chance was gone. In mid-October Premier Tilley had feigned great surprise and hurt – despite the fact that he had informed his lieutenant-governor, Gordon, of the true state of affairs as early as 2 February 1863 – when Sandfield officially asked for new negotiations on the rail line.

34 2 Oct. 1863.
35 Brown Papers, Brown to Anne Brown, 28 Sept. 1863.
36 *QM*, 13 Oct. 1863.

New Brunswick refused to participate in the survey. To show good faith, when Britain refused to back the survey, without colonial agreement, Sandfield had Canada unilaterally finance Sandford Fleming. Still the New Brunswick recriminations checked Sandfield's growing prestige. It further deteriorated with an argument between Brown and Holton over the latter's removal of government accounts from the tory but weak Bank of Upper Canada to the Bank of Montreal and Holton's reluctance to spend long weeks in Washington trying to save the Reciprocity Treaty of 1854, while his fiscal reform measures would be up for debate in the Assembly. Brown, who refused himself to go to Washington, was also annoyed at Sandfield's selection of A. N. Richards, an eastern Baldwinite, as the new solicitor general west. Furthermore, he vetoed Sandfield's efforts to bolster his sagging strength by securing through patronage the support of several of the notorius 'loose fish' of the Ottawa valley.[37] Meanwhile Foley and McGee were publicly attacking the premier's integrity.

On the external scene there was likewise no relief. Across the border the war raged on, and with Northern victories at Vicksburg and Gettysburg, the Yankees' enmity against Britain intensified as the havoc caused by the British-built *Alabama* and other Confederate raiders seemed to be prolonging the struggle. When relations between Washington and London deteriorated, the Yankee threat to Canada increased. Although Sandfield, through personal contacts with General Dix in Buffalo, had frustrated a Confederate raid in November from Canada to release prisoners of war on Johnson Island and although through contacts with Seward he had had McDougall be present for Lincoln's Gettysburg address, congressional animosity to things British seemed bound to give American protectionists the opportunity of abrogating the Reciprocity Treaty. Such action would have been a great economic and especially political blow to Sandfield's régime. Meanwhile, the pessimistic Colonel Jervois of the War Office was in Canada preparing a negative report on the possibilities of imperial defence of Upper Canada. During the Christmas vacation Sandfield had conferred with Seward in New York, but local politics, this time the South Leeds by-election in which John A. Macdonald and McGee took personal charge to defeat A. N. Richards, had again

37 Brown Papers, Brown to Anne Brown, 22 Feb. 1864.

prevented him from going on to Washington and engaging in genuine personal diplomacy.[38]

Meanwhile, Sandfield and finance minister Holton, backed by John Langton, the crusading provincial auditor, prepared their forward-looking Audit Bill. This measure, which lacked any British precedent, was undoubtedly Sandfield's greatest legislative achievement. Once enacted into law, it 'marked a revolution in the method of internal and external financial control'[39] and a most decisive step in establishing 'effective responsible government in public expenditure.'[40] The Board of Audit was expanded and given the task of determining the system of audit, and the auditor rather than the deputy minister of finance became its chairman and chief officer. He was to ensure that no warrants were paid for expenditure without parliamentary approval, except those of the governor-in-council issued between sessions for emergency repairs on buildings. Henceforth, the minister of finance was required to submit estimates to parliament in advance. The bill as passed failed to place the auditor directly under parliament rather than under the executive; despite this shortcoming, Langton was incorruptible.

The bill was a fitting triumph for a Baldwinite, but in the winter of 1864 it was not yet on the statute books. Parliament opened on 19 February 1864. The government hoped to secure passage of the audit bill and Holton's new tax bill quickly. The opposition, however, sensing that its moment was near, virtually talked the Assembly to a halt. For thirteen hours Cartier castigated the government, and then a few days later sent Christine, who again was in town with her husband, a charming letter enclosing his *chanson* '*O Canada, mon pays, mes amours.*'[41]

In political desperation, Sandfield approached respected old Sir Etienne Taché of the upper house on the possibility of a coalition of Baldwinite and Hincksite Reformers and moderate Conservatives,

38 Seward Collection, JSM to Seward, 31 Dec. 1863.
39 J. E. Hodgetts, *Pioneer Public Service: An Administrative History of the United Canadas, 1841–1867* (Toronto 1955), p. 107.
40 Norman Ward, *The Public Purse: A Study in Canadian Democracy* (Toronto 1962), p. 36.
41 Brown Papers, Brown to Anne Brown, 1 March 1864, and JSM Papers, Cartier to Christine Macdonald, 5 March 1864.

including John A. but excluding Cartier. Both Taché and Monck were interested, but Sandfield's offer of two of the six cabinet posts for Conservatives in Upper Canada and four of the six posts in Lower Canada was not enough.[42] It was all over. On 21 March, Dorion tendered Sandfield his resignation and that of his Lower Canadian colleagues. The same day, Sandfield submitted his own resignation to Monck. Had he waited for a fully attended division, the premier from Cornwall would probably have lost by one vote. Nevertheless, the Upper Canadian Reform caucus voted unqualified confidence in him as leader and appreciation of his conduct as premier.[43]

The Reform schisms, demonstrated clearly during the debate and vote on the Scott bill, had finally done their damage. Sectionalism, sectarianism, prejudice, and small mindedness, coupled with the political astuteness of the Opposition and the climate of the Civil War, had destroyed Sandfield's premiership and with it the great Reform vision. Taxation reform was lost, and Sandfield's audit bill would receive royal assent under Taché's premiership.

42 *LFP*, 5 and 6 April 1864, and W. L. Morton, *The Critical Years: The Union of British North America, 1857–1873* (Toronto 1964), pp. 141–43.
43 *QM*, 25 March 1864.

5

On the Sidelines

Between March 1864 and Confederation, events and his own inclinations thrust Sandfield Macdonald to the sidelines of history. In the spring of 1864 a Conservative Taché régime finally succeeded Sandfield's; it was as unstable as its predecessor. On 14 June it was defeated by two votes on a motion by Dorion and McDougall. The same day, a constitutional committee, long sought for and chaired by Brown, resolved in favour of constitutional change 'in the direction of a Federative system, applied either to Canada alone, or to the whole British North American Provinces.' Twelve men signed the report, including Brown, Cartier, McDougall, Holton, McGee and Mowat. Five members of the commitee, including Dorion, were absent. Three signed in rejection of the report: John Scoble, John A. Macdonald and John Sandfield Macdonald. Ordinary party politics in Canada had reached the end of the road. The report and the fall of the government set off a chain reaction leading to the temporary reconciliation of Brown with Cartier and John A. and the formation of the Great Coalition pledged to work for employing the federal principle either to unify all British North America or failing that to reorganize the Province of Canada. There followed the intensive summer discussions among members of the coalition, the meeting with Maritime delegates at Charlottetown, the drawing up of the 72 Resolutions at the Quebec conference, and the presentation of these Resolutions to the Canadian legislature in February, 1865. In all of these stirring events Sandfield played no role. He could take some small consolation from the fact that on 30 June, 1864, the day the Great Coalition was formally sworn in, his administratively significant audit bill received Monck's signature. Such a measure was not, however, the popular stuff of nation-building.

Sandfield still remained for many of his countrymen a controversial or enigmatic figure. The *Canadian Illustrated News* described him as a man of 'frail health' with an austere disposition and a severe caste of mind, yet one who, with his wife and children, was noted for his generous hospitality. His 'fortunate investment in landed property' had given him great personal freedom and independence; a proud admirer of Baldwin, he fully accepted the essential diversity of the Canadian population.[1] Blackburn described him as a truly great, courageous and selfless Reformer, dedicated to the progress of his country.[2] Egerton Ryerson, who normally distrusted Reformers, was unstinting in his praise for Sandfield's ability and for the generous hospitality he and his wife had extended to Ryerson's unhappy daughter Sophie, the close friend of their eldest daughter Louise; Ryerson said that he could never hope to rival his friend's hospitality at Ivy Hall 'as to wines, etc.,' nor would it be 'becoming my profession or character to do so.'[3] Yet John A., Ryerson's other great political friend, was still describing Sandfield as a 'base bad man.'[4] Brown had no confidence in either Sandfield's ability or his integrity; Holton had misgivings. The aristocratic Hincksite Sydney Smith told John A. that Sandfield had lapses in political integrity because he had reached an exalted position 'to which he was not entitled either by birth, standing, education, intelligence, ability or character.'[5]

Perhaps the most revealing commentary on Sandfield at this point in his life came from a mellow George Brown. Writing to his wife after attending a small dinner party at the Sandfields' in Quebec, in February 1864, Brown noted that he had found himself alone with Christine and her three vivacious elder daughters. They talked ever so frankly of love and marriage, military, town and country life,

1 *Canadian Illustrated News*, 31 Jan. 1863.
2 *QM*, 22 March 1864.
3 C. B. Sissons, ed., *My Dearest Sophie: Letters of Egerton Ryerson to his Daughter* (Toronto 1955), pp. 54–61, Ryerson to Sophie, 15, 16, 27 July 1864, and 1 Aug. 1864.
4 Macdonald Papers, Macdonald to S. Amsden, 25 Dec. 1863.
5 *Ibid.*, Smith to Macdonald, Oct. 1864.

dancing and nunneries. Josephine planned to marry a tolerable man for money. Just as the host entered the room, Brown was asserting that his greatest enjoyment came from sitting pleasantly with his wife while she held their tiny child. Christine was astonished and impressed. She claimed that she never thought such a man existed. At this, Sandfield scoffed and departed, claiming that the talk was merely 'soft sawder for the ladies.' Later Christine asserted that her daughters 'never stood in the presence of their father without fear, and never spoke a word to him in confidence in their lives.'[6] Yet despite Brown's testimony, Sandfield was, by Victorian standards, a good, provident, if aloof father and certainly a faithful, considerate husband. An enigma to many, a villain to a few, and a selfless Canadian leader to others, he was a politician who in many respects understood his diverse and changing Province of Canada better than did most other Reformers.

On 3 February, 1865, the Canadian government submitted the Quebec Resolutions to the legislature for approval. Immediately and without success, Sandfield, backed by Holton, objected to the procedure whereby the Assembly would deal exclusively with the Resolutions until a verdict was rendered. The 'outrageously strong' coalition was attempting to ram through drastic constitutional changes before the people had a chance to reflect and to express their verdict.[7] As titular leader of the opposition, he appeared frustrated and at first only participated in debate through short, cryptic and sarcastic interjections. He backed Dorion's attack on the nefarious political power of the Grand Trunk in pushing Confederation so as to get its hands on the projected Intercolonial railway.[8] When Cartier and English-speaking Lower Canadian Conservatives implied that they planned later to introduce a measure to remove certain anomalies in the position of the Protestant minority of Lower Canada with regard to dissentient schools, Sandfield raised a query. All admitted that generally the Protestant minority had a combined legal and pragmatic position vastly superior to the Catholic minority in Upper Canada and that Lower Canada had never had a schools crisis. But how would Brown and others react to new demands for equal treatment

6 Brown Papers, Brown to Anne Brown, 23 Feb. 1864.
7 *Conf. Debates*, pp. 13–14.
8 *Ibid.*, p. 25.

by the Catholics of Upper Canada?[9] Repeatedly Sandfield also tried to find out what defence projects for British North America were planned and at what cost to Canada. On the core question, his position was summarized by the interjection 'Leave us as we are.'[10] He unleashed a lengthy procedural furore (not officially reported) when he informed the house that Joseph Cauchon, veteran Bleu from the Quebec City area, had pulled the nose of Alexandre Dufresne, a Rouge, during a heated exchange behind the speaker's chair.[11] Sandfield also had great fun interrupting the speech by Colonel Haultain, Conservative from Peterborough; Haultain's oration proved to be an embarrassment to Cartier because of its anti-papist outbursts and loud protestations of concern for the fate of the Lower Canadian minority. Sandfield also ridiculed the colonel, and through him the government, for using a Little England article from the *Edinburgh Review* as support for the Quebec scheme. Knowing the article, Sandfield gleefully noted that its concluding thesis argued for Confederation as a step toward full separation from Britain and thus the dissolution of the Empire.[12]

His first real speech, however, came on 6 March,[13] after John A. announced the defeat of Tilley's pro-Confederation forces in the New Brunswick election and the Canadian government's resolve to press on with renewed vigour, dealing with the Resolutions 'as a treaty to be endorsed without one single amendment or alteration.' The government would then prorogue the legislature and send delegates to Britain to discuss defence, the Intercolonial and Confederation. The implication was clear that somehow New Brunswickers would be pressured into changing their minds. Sandfield was at his vengeful and liberal best. His namesake was chastised for indecent haste, inconsistency and high-handed intentions; Brown was chided for not coming forward now with his 'pet scheme,' the federation of old Canada; and Tilley was gleefully depicted as suffering just retributive justice. If New Brunswick contained many American annexationists, as some Conservative organs claimed in explaining the defeat and as he doubted, then Canada should declare 'a day of general thanks-

9 *Ibid.*, pp. 412 and 418–21.
10 *Ibid.*, p. 477.
11 Brown Papers, Brown to Anne Brown, 1 and 2 March 1864.
12 *Conf. Debates*, pp. 631–33.
13 *Ibid.*, pp. 650–54.

giving' for escaping combination with them. If New Brunswickers were susceptible to bribes, which he doubted, then 'we must presume that they are not of the race of British freemen who, elsewhere, would resent with indignation – ay rebel – before yielding up their independence'; if they were such then they were 'unworthy of association with us.' Above all, the election results, in which 'Tilley and his followers were routed horse and foot by the honest people,' showed the folly of governments taking action not authorized by their legislatures or acceptable to their electorates. Sandfield took the greatest 'mischievous pleasure' in seeing the scoundrel Tilley, 'this betrayer of the trust of the people, ... disposed of by the people.' Tilley had dared accuse Sandfield when premier of breaking faith on the Intercolonial, when he knew full well that the 1862 agreement would have to be re-negotiated and that he, Sandfield, was a great believer in the desirability of the rail line. With its Quebec scheme doomed, what did the government intend, at a time when the minds of Canadians had been 'unhinged' and political parties 'demoralized'? What costly defence expenditures would be agreed to in London?

'Sir,' he concluded, 'I never was myself an advocate of any change in our Constitution; I believed it was capable of being well worked to the satisfaction of the people, if we were free from demagogues and designing persons who sought to create strife between the sections.' In this he had a partial point. Had British and Canadian pressures, the backlash from the Fenian schemes, and the designing efforts of the minority pro-Confederation leadership in the Maritimes not ultimately triumphed, the old Province of Canada could possibly have survived with some political rearrangement for several more years. An auspicious moment for somewhat differently reorganizing British North America might then have presented itself. The Quebec scheme as such was neither inevitably successful nor necessarily essential for the survival and prosperity of the provinces and territories.

Later the same day, Sandfield re-entered the debate with further accusations. If the Resolutions were approved, ministers would go to Britain and argue that they had *carte blanche* from the people. They would return with a modified scheme, including in it costly defence expenditures and the local constitutions for Upper and Lower Canada; this would be choked down the throats of Canadians by imperial statute, as was done in 1840. John A., in an angry response which insulted the intelligence, integrity, loyalty and eloquence of his opponent, now pledged that the legislature, later in 1865, would consider the local constitutions, defence projects, reciprocity, the schools question and any changes in the Quebec scheme. Sandfield proudly remarked that the insults which he had just sustained were a small price to pay for at least securing that commitment, although he himself favoured at this time neither a federal nor a legislative union with the Maritimes.[14]

The next day he delivered his major and rather rambling address against Confederation.[15] Technically directed against John A.'s attempt to gag debate by moving 'the previous question,' it argued that the coalition was seriously curtailing Canadian autonomy and selling out popular rights. The scheme would lead to vast expenditures on defence and withdrawals of men from productive labour, both of which Canada could ill afford when suffering from severe economic and financial difficulties. British authorities, alarmed by the pessimistic Little Englanders, were increasing pressure on Canada, and he feared that ministers would not be as resistant as his government had been. He resented the 'gratuitous insult' which with 'buncombe talk' imputed disloyalty or annexationism to anyone who opposed the Quebec plan. Native-born Canadians were particularly 'anxious to keep their hearths and firesides free from the pollution of the invader,' and it was often arrivals of 'yesterday' who had the 'audacity' to question loyalty. Nevertheless, Canada could repel a determined American invasion only with massive British aid, and the now happily declining threat arose primarily because Canada was part of the British Empire. Confederation, with its American-style institutions, the antithesis of retrenchment, the illegitimate child of the Little Englanders, might even by impoverishing Canada promote the very annexationism most everyone abhorred. In describing the economic ills which beset the country, he revealed the degree to which he differed from Brown on economic policy. Vehemently opposing Brown's 'free trade in money,' which around Cornwall endangered the 'family homestead,' he showed himself to be less the liberal capitalist and more the farmers' and merchants' lawyer and the successful stable investor. 'Our wealth is in our lands, where we own but little money,' he re-

14 *Ibid.*, pp. 662–67.
15 *Ibid.*, pp. 720–42.

peated, and this year, one of poor harvest, the farmer and retailer were caught with huge debt charges, the legacy of Brown's successful removal of the usury laws in 1853. Coming amid the railway boom of the fifties, this measure had allowed interest rates on mortgages and other loans to soar uncontrolled; simple folk were now paying exhorbitant rates, even as high as 30 or 40 per cent, often merely to pay on loans obtained at only slightly lower rates. Who benefited from all this? Not many Canadians, because dividends primarily were flowing out of the country to owners of 'the moneyed corporations' that were attracted by the 'usurious rates of interest.' Despite valiant efforts he had never been able to re-establish controls, and now the indebted farmer was being led to see Confederation as a solution to his ills, when in fact it would raise his taxes.

On 10 March 1865, by a vote of 91 to 33, the legislative assembly approved the Quebec Resolutions with a double majority. Thanks to the Rouges, the vote was rather close in Lower Canada. From Upper Canada only six Reformers, including Donald, and one Conservative, M. C. Cameron, voted with Sandfield. Furthermore, two or three of the other five were spokesmen for the narrow sectional and anti-French old Clear Grit position; they thus had little in common with their leader. On 13 March Sandfield continued the fight, enthusiastically backing the move by two renegade Conservatives, J. H. Cameron and M. C. Cameron, to secure an electoral appeal before final imperial implementation. In parts Sandfield's speech was almost eloquent:

Sir, it has been my misfortune to have been nearly nineteen years of my political life in the cold shades of opposition, but I am satisfied to stay an infinitely longer period on this side of the House, if that shall be the effect of my contending for the views which I have just expressed. I have always believed that I was here for the purpose of representing the constituency which sent me, and not for the purpose of misrepresenting them. If I were satisfied that I did not properly represent my constituency on any leading question coming before this House, I would scorn to sit here a moment longer than was absolutely necessary, until I could do so by their approval. But, sir, are there not members here who know full well that their conduct has been condemned by their constituents in the most unmistakable man-

ner? And yet these hon. members rise up and express their virtuous indignation at our contending that the people should have a voice in reference to the adoption of this new Constitution ... If there has been one question more than another before this House, for the last quarter of a century, upon which the views of the people, ought to be clearly and distinctly ascertained, it is upon this proposal to destroy the Constitution; and if gentlemen will vote against it, then I hope that at the next general election, the people will pass such a judgement upon them as well as prevent any such scheme ever being proposed in any British Colonial Legislature, without the sanction of the people, during all future time.[16]

In contrast, Brown ridiculed the notion of a popular appeal and called the idea 'an insult' to the queen and the imperial parliament.[17] If not quite a democrat, Sandfield was closer to being one than was his great antagonist who feared 'the ignorant unreasoning mass.'[18]

Soon after this 'democratic' motion had failed 35 to 84, Sandfield moved that the new local legislatures be given full control over education, 'subject only to the approval or disapproval of the General Parliament.'[19] If this had passed, it would have removed the perpetual guarantee of separate and dissentient school rights as they existed at the time of Confederation but would have suited John A.'s philosophy of having the central parliament as the guarantor of minority rights. 'A denial of the right of the majority to legislate on any given matter,' Sandfield argued, 'has always led to grave consequences' and he alluded to the clergy reserves as a cause of the Upper Canadian Rebellion of 1837 and slavery as a factor in the American Civil War. Besides, to deny a specific power to a majority tends to make that power a forbidden fruit which must be tasted. 'The minority will be quite safe on a question relating to their faith and their education in a colony under the sway of the British Crown' and the 'sense of justice' of most Upper Canadians. Perhaps Alexander Mackenzie was partly right when he argued that Sandfield was mainly trying to tempt pro-Confederation Grits to desert Brown. If so, only two were tempted. Even the Rouges lacked faith in the majority's

16 *Ibid.*, pp. 1012–13.
17 *Ibid.*, p. 992.
18 *Globe*, 23 Sept. 1857.
19 *Conf. Debates*, p. 1020.

sense of justice. The motion received only eight votes, all Upper Canadian. Thereupon Sandfield became the only Upper Canadian to vote for a Rouge motion extending to Catholics in Upper Canada the same rights enjoyed by Protestants in Lower Canada.[20] Thus ended the prophetic Confederation debates.

A few days later, after reluctantly joining with the majority in voting up to one million dollars for permanent fortifications, Sandfield was injured in a traffic accident, which, he reported, 'came near finishing me.'[21] He was taken home to Ivy Hall to convalesce. Before returning to Quebec in August for the short summer session, he enjoyed time for family relaxation and for attention to his private affairs. He arranged for more effective management of the *Freeholder*. He also supervised the construction on his growing land holdings in St Andrews, north of Cornwall, of a large three-storey stone hotel. On a business trip to Toronto, he saw Anne Brown but failed to learn from her anything about what her husband and his colleagues were up to in London.[22] Back in Quebec he participated in the debate on the London mission and was pleased that no commitments had been made for costly defence installations. He supported the government's bill to expand secondary education in Upper Canada; it was really Ryerson's bill, and Sandfield had worked for it when premier. But his heart seemed back with his people. On St Andrew's Day (30th November) at St Andrews, in his still unopened hotel, he threw the largest party of his life, for the young people of the area. With 600 and 700 'lads and lasses' dancing Scottish reels on two floors, some 'till broad day light,' with one vivacious daughter in charge of dispensing delightful edibles and 'the cup that cheers but not inebriates,' and with his seventeen-year-old son Henry giving 'the most assiduous attention to the guests,' some of the elder generation betook themselves to a farm house on his property, and 'enlivened by the flowing bowl' sang Gaelic airs for hours.[23] The host had found great pleasure in the happiness of the people he had grown up amongst and whose interests were his. Christine, however, was absent. With

20 *Ibid.*, pp. 1025–27.
21 JSM Papers, JSM to A. MacLean, 25 March 1865.
22 Brown Papers, Brown to Anne Brown, 10 June 1865.
23 *Freeholder*, 8 Dec. 1865.

the guns now silent in the South, she was on an extended visit to the Waggamans in New Orleans and did not return until late spring 1866.

By then the political situation in the provinces had again changed. In Cornwall local Conservatives and Grits had combined to defeat Sandfield's candidate for mayor, but their subsequent pro-government dinner, aimed at embarrassing Sandfield, misfired. In anger Brown had left the coalition in December 1865 but his lieutenants, McDougall and Howland, had refused to follow suit. John A., Galt and Howland used the rather poorly attended dinner to attack the absent Brown, thus splitting the local Grits. Meanwhile, the Fenian scare was increasing. Sandfield had the *Freeholder* urge the populace to be ever on guard to repulse attack, while Donald, as senior officer of the four Glengarry militia battalions, eagerly readied himself for duty. On the constitutional issue, Sandfield continued to argue against seeing the choice as one between Confederation and annexation. The present British-style constitution was viable, and at the auspicious moment, after railways were built and natural contacts increased, the present union could with the will of the people be extended both eastward and westward. It was not union but the arbitrary haste and the extravagant federal nature of the Quebec scheme that he opposed.[24]

Before the legislature met on 8 June 1866, for its last session, but its first in Ottawa, the New Brunswick government had broken up, and the new one under Peter Mitchell and Tilley, pledged to union with Canada, had won its election; in Nova Scotia Tupper had secured vague legislative authorization to continue Confederation negotiations. On the Niagara frontier, Canadian militiamen, with considerable loss, had repulsed a Fenian invasion. At the session, Sandfield's opposition mellowed. Initially, he tried vainly with Dorion to have an electoral appeal precede major constitutional change; again he argued for a legislative union of British North America in the future. But the main business concerned the proposed constitutions for the future Ontario and Quebec and the educational rights of their respective minorities. Claiming that if provinces were to have lieutenant governors the people should have some say in their selection, he clashed head on with Brown; Brown agreed with John A.'s plan to have them appointed by the federal government. Brown also

24 *Ibid.*, 2, 9, 16, 23, 30 March and 6 April 1866.

argued, as he had in 1864, that the new subordinate provinces should have only a simple, county-like structure rather than a full parliamentary system. Like most Reformers, Sandfield agreed that Ontario should have no upper house. He accepted the modest reduction in tariffs to accommodate Maritimers, but with Conservatives he opposed the doctrine of free trade. He again voiced concern that Catholics in Upper Canada would feel inferior if the government went through with its plan to extend the educational rights of Protestants in Lower Canada. When the anticipated bill was introduced, R. Bell of Russell countered with one which would have extended the same rights to Upper Canadian Catholics. Both Brownite and government Grits were equally in an uproar as were many Conservatives. Though John A. and John Sandfield would reluctantly have accepted both bills, John A. withdrew the government measure, Galt, the champion of the Protestants of Lower Canada, resigned, and the status quo survived. Sandfield was extremely pleased with this reversal. He was also delighted when the Assembly agreed to his suggestion that it provide $500 to purchase a bust of his hero, Robert Baldwin.[25] On 15 August the Canadian legislature ended forever, and as Sandfield returned the short distance to Cornwall, he seemed now to accept Confederation as inevitable and to be more or less reconciled to it even though its governmental structure shattered the unity of the St Lawrence and Ottawa valleys and the unity of his beloved central Canada.

During the next few quiet months in Cornwall, Sandfield's thoughts centred on what his own role should be in the new scheme of things. What should his relationship be to the coalition and to the disunited Reformers? Holton, that brilliant Unitarian who now accepted Confederation and proposed reforming it later, re-established his old friendship with Brown and, moderating Dorion, was working for the creation of a national Liberal party; Brown was trying to gather up the pieces of Upper Canadian liberalism by means of another great convention, and at the same time joining with other Liberals in the formation of a large Toronto financial institution, the Bank of Commerce. Brown and Holton both opposed the coalition, the former

25 *Globe*, 14 and 28 July and 1, 3, 11 Aug. 1866; *Leader*, 11 and 28 July and 8 Aug. 1866; Canadian Library Association, *Parliamentary Debates*, 17 July and 2 Aug. 1866.

being particularly bitter about the continued presence in it of McDougall and Howland, and the latter being worried about Sandfield's contacts with these two former colleagues.

On 29 March 1867 the British North America Act received royal assent. For Sandfield the crucial moment was approaching. In April, D. A. Macdonald (Sandfield), assuring Brown that he vehemently opposed the coalition and favoured a real British American union, urged the *Globe* editor to reverse his decision not to run personally for election.[26] Because Holton had urged Brown to strengthen his eastern flank, Brown thought that it might be a coup to have Donald as chairman of the convention.[27] But on 8 and 9 May, John Sandfield was in Ottawa on legal business; John A. had arrived there a few days earlier to commence negotiations to launch the new ship of state on 1 July. In the capital, the Cornwall Macdonald was the house guest of the Kingston Macdonald. Leaving Ottawa by steamer,[28] Sandfield soon found himself in Montreal having talks and dinner with Galt. Nevertheless, he also met Holton several times, and although he admitted to advising McDougall and Howland not to leave the coalition until a good pretext emerged, he assured him of his permanent dedication to the Reform cause. Holton told Brown that he worried lest John A. tempt Sandfield with the office of lieutenant governor of Ontario.[29]

On 5 June McDougall successfully made his proposals to John A. for continued coalition at the new federal level.[30] The prime minister-elect also planned to establish coalition rule in Ontario, and for this endeavour he had the close co-operation of both McDougall and Howland. T. C. Wallbridge, the oppositionist closest to the Sandfields, soon indicated his intention to support coalition.[31] Donald Sandfield stayed away from Brown's Reform convention held from 27 to 29 June in Toronto; chaired instead by Patrick of Grenville South, it overwhelmingly rejected coalition and ousted McDougall and Howland from the Reform Association. A jubilant Brown again overestimated the importance of a managed convention, but even he

26 Brown Papers, DAM to Brown, 18 April 1867.
27 *Ibid.*, Brown to Holton, 19 June 1867.
28 *Globe*, 10 May 1867.
29 Brown Papers, Holton to Brown, 16 May 1867.
30 Macdonald Papers, McDougall to Macdonald, 5 June 1867.
31 Brown Papers, John Climie to Brown, 16 May 1867.

worried about Sandfield and the Grit weakness in central Canada.[32] On the day that the convention assembled, senator-elect D. L. Macpherson, John A.'s principal confidant in Toronto, warned his chief that Major General Stisted, who would soon be Ontario's provisional lieutenant governor and who was totally inexperienced in politics, would have to be instructed on exactly what he should do and whom he should summon as advisers. Macpherson urged John A. to have the whole Ontario coalition cabinet set up quickly, so that the Brownites would appear as a mere faction.[33] Two days after the first Dominion Day, he again wrote to his chief, now Sir John. 'Sandfield would undoubtedly be the best Premier,' he stated, apparently in answer to a suggestion from Sir John, 'if he would accept it and do his work fairly. He, Howland and McDougall could choose two Reform colleagues and you should [choose] the two Conservatives.'[34]

On 4 July Sandfield was in Montreal assuring Holton 'of his avowed increasing attachment to the liberal cause,' but he urged the Rouges not to make any pre-election pacts with the Brownites and hinted that he might receive an offer which would not involve service under Sir John. Using 'soft sawder,' Holton told Sandfield that he was the man best placed to become Liberal prime minister of Canada after the election. The next day Sandfield made a hurried visit to Ottawa. On 8 July he was again in Montreal warning Dorion and Holton that he now anticipated an invitation to head the Ontario ministry. Having thought of the lieutenant governorship or a high federal post as the only offices which Sandfield would ever consider, Holton was shocked and had faint hope 'that they had dissuaded him.' Dorion had none.[35] The same day, with Hewitt Bernard, Sir John's secretary and brother-in-law, as meticulous coach and Senator Macpherson in the background, General Stisted wrote to Sandfield in Cornwall asking him to attempt to form an administration. Receiving the note on 9 July, Sandfield merely replied that he would come up to Toronto to discuss the matter.[36] On his way that day, he had further discussions with Sir John in Prescott, and on the morrow

32 Mackenzie Papers, Brown to Holton, 2 July 1867.
33 Macdonald Papers, 27 July 1867.
34 *Ibid.*, 29 July 1867.
35 Brown Papers, Holton to Brown, 4 July 1867 and Brown to Holton, 10 July 1867, and *Globe*, 6 July 1867.
36 JSM Papers, Stisted to JSM, 8 July 1867 and JSM to Stisted, 9 July 1867.

accepted the invitation.[37] He spent the next few days cabinet building in Toronto, St Catharines and elsewhere. When Sir John came up to help, the publisher of the *Globe* was furious, in the full knowledge that hated coalition was inevitable.[38]

On 15 July John Sandfield Macdonald, the gaunt, lanky liberal Catholic Baldwinite from central Canada, became the first premier of Ontario when he was sworn in as attorney general. The same day, John Carling, the progressive Conservative brewer from London, became commissioner of agriculture and public works and the unknown and totally inexperienced Stephen Richards, brother of the Baldwinite defeated in 1864, became commissioner of crown lands. Five days later, Sandfield filled the remaining cabinet posts. The Brantford Reformer Edmund Burke Wood, who liked to be called 'Big Thunder' but was said to be 'owned' by the railway interests,[39] became provincial secretary, and M. C. Cameron, the tory who had opposed Confederation, became provincial treasurer. The premier had encountered considerable difficulty in finding two suitable Reformers. Richards and Woods were neither first choices nor strong leaders. Here lay the weakness. In 1863 Upper Canadians had indicated clearly that a large majority of voters favoured the Reformers. Yet in 1867 who represented the cause of Reform: Brown's 'faction' or Sandfield's 'Patent Combination'?

37 *Globe*, 10 July 1867, and Macdonald Papers, Macdonald to Gibbs, 11 July 1867.
38 *Globe*, 15 and 17 July 1867.
39 Brown Papers, Brown to Holton, 2 July 1867.

6

'What the Hell has Strathroy Done for Me?'

The humble lad from Glengarry, the proud and sickly lawyer from Cornwall, was now first minister of the crown in Ontario. Regarded by the Grits as a 'political Judas, ... ambitious without talent,'[1] Sandfield remained in fact and in sentiment a Reformer. In the hot, sultry summer of 1867, Sandfield's principal task was to have confirmed at the polls what he and Sir John had constructed at the executive level. It was an unique election. In Ontario, Quebec and Nova Scotia voting for the federal and provincial contests was run together on the same two days in each constituency; it was still the practice, however, to have the election dates vary from riding to riding. In many Ontario constituencies there were in fact three party organizations, the Grit Reformers, the Coalition Reformers, and the Conservatives. The two first ministers 'hunted in pairs.' Each of them criss-crossed the province many times and wrote dozens of letters to iron out difficulties and to see to it that Coalition Reformers and Conservatives did not run against one another, despite years of past animosity. In one riding where a Conservative candidate seemed strong Sandfield would persuade a Coalition Reformer bent on a federal seat to settle for a provincial one. In another Sir John would attempt the same result with a Conservative. Then both leaders and their lieutenants would urge their followers to regard the resulting compromise as a binding ticket. Often a strong federal candidate pulled in a weak provincial one, frequently a man from the rival part of the coalition. The work

1 *London Advertiser*, 18 Dec. 1868.

was productive. The euphoria of Confederation, the dreams of nation-building, the continued aggressive talk of Americans, the habit of three years of McDougall–John A. Macdonald coalition, the advantages accruing to the two governments as managers of the electoral machinery, and the over-confidence and frustrated disarray of the Brownites, all played their part in the victory.[2]

Never campaigning harder, Sandfield travelled and spoke so much that the *Globe* claimed that his behaviour was demagogic, denigrating to his high office, and most un-British; the *Leader* replied that this was Canada and not England.[3] When the results were in, he took the greatest satisfaction from the knowledge of how poorly the opposition had done in eastern Ontario, but clearly the Conservatives were gaining more than the Coalition Reformers. Even in his United Counties the federal member returned by acclamation for Dundas was a Conservative; so was William Colquhoun, the provincial member elected for Stormont. Glengarry's provincial member, James Craig, like Stormant's federal member, was a Coalition Reformer, but Donald's election by acclamation for the federal seat for Glengarry was ominous; tension between the two brothers was rising again as Donald had kept his ties with Brown and had not clearly endorsed coalition; in this regard Sandfield had been nervous enough to prevent his former legal protegé, A. M. MacKenzie, now county registrar and still a Brownite, from being the returning officer.[4] In Cornwall, Sandfield easily defeated his federal and his provincial Grit challengers, and in October he was pleased that his colleagues of the Cornwall bar were not too divided by politics to request and secure permission to have his portrait painted. Sandfield was not too happy about the Ottawa situation where R. W. Scott won the provincial seat. He had had enough trouble with that lumber baron, whose economic as well as political empire clashed with the empire of the Sandfield family, and yet he had not dared to campaign for Scott's Reform opponent who pledged to support Sandfield. In Leeds South, the Conservatives had refused to withdraw in favour of Albert

2 Numerous letters in the JSM Papers and the Macdonald Papers give evidence of all these influences. Note also Helen Small, 'Federal and Provincial Election Campaigns in Ontario, 1867' (unpublished master's thesis, Queen's Univ., 1968).

3 *Globe*, 5 and 10 Sept. 1867, and *Leader* (weekly), 20 Sept. 1867.

4 *Globe*, 16 Aug. 1867.

and Stephen Richards, and the animosity of the 1864 by-election had been too bitter for the two chief ministers to sort out. The Richards were defeated. Sir John A. and Macpherson helped Sandfield secure a safe seat for his commissioner of crown lands in a by-election that December in Niagara.

Sandfield could rejoice in the fact that George Brown's career as an active practising politician was at an end. Rejecting the Grit chieftain, the voters of the South Riding of the county of Ontario re-elected, for the federal seat, the Conservative T. N. Gibbs. Sandfield, McDougall, and M. C. Cameron all made forays into the Oshawa area, and Sir John had worked in the background. Brown told his wife that Sandfield had 'made an ass of himself' in the riding, but the coalition had held.[5] Brown had chosen this marginal constituency to strengthen his weak eastern flank, and he resolutely refused to secure a safe seat elsewhere.

In the provincial contest, Brown's two chief lieutenants, Adam Crooks and Archibald McKellar, went down to defeat, although McKellar soon secured an alternative seat. Also defeated was the bitter Michael Foley; he had swung back to the Brownites so that he could oppose Sandfield, who thereupon campaigned against him, 'using the wildest language' and swearing 'by his Maker and his Saviour,' it was claimed.[6] These defeats raised the prestige in opposition ranks of the brilliant, but unmanageable Edward Blake, who like Sandfield secured election to both the Legislative Assembly and the House of Commons. McKellar became the leader of the opposition in Toronto, and Alexander Mackenzie the Brownite leader in Ottawa, but the man to watch was Edward Blake, the intellectual son of the aristocrat whose elevation to the bench in 1849 had enabled Sandfield to become Baldwin's solicitor general west.

The premier was pleased, too, that the Catholic vote did not go to the opposition. Frank Smith, wealthy mayor of London, had organized a July convention in Toronto aimed at 'securing united political action' by Catholics against the coalition[7]; before accepting office, Sandfield had planned to attend and attempt to dissuade delegates

5 Brown Papers, 25 July 1867.
6 Clarke Papers, Foley to Clarke, 8 Aug. 1867, and Macdonald Papers, JSM to Macdonald, 13 Aug. 1867.
7 JSM Papers, form letter from Frank Smith *et al.* to JSM, 21 June 1867, plus numerous letters on this subject in the JSM and Macdonald Papers.

from the proposed object, but the movement had proved largely abortive anyway.

Sandfield was happy to have again the warm backing of both the Toronto *Leader* and Josiah Blackburn's London *Free Press*. Blackburn had declined to back his old friend's opposition to Confederation and was still somewhat embarrassingly suggesting that Confederation should be followed by friendly separation from the British empire and by internationally guaranteed neutrality on the Belgian model. Nevertheless his support was gratifying.

Another slight embarrassment to Sandfield came from the thesis advanced by certain friends of coalition that party government was wrong. The *Leader* claimed that a long period of combination was necessary to add flesh to the skeleton of the British North America Act; later, new logical divisions would appear.[8] The Canadian prime minister himself was most adept at defending 'the Union ticket' and denouncing the principle of party as 'the madness of many for the good of a few.'[9] Sir John also pointed out privately that without the 'bold' Sandfield, 'the whole province would have been governed by a Grit Government.'[10] Ryerson, the influential chief superintendent of education in Ontario and a close friend of both first ministers, fully identified with the coalition cause. He published just before the election a pamphlet entitled *The New Canadian Dominion: Dangers and Duties of the People in Regard to their Government*. This highly conservative and provocative document, which quoted liberally from English sages of bygone eras and enraged the *Globe*,[11] denounced permanent political parties as un-British, factious, wasteful, irresponsible, immoral, and conducive to a decline in 'religious feelings.' It described Sandfield Macdonald as 'a plain, sensible, impartial man, whose private life is above suspicion; and whom envy itself has never dared to accuse of having used political power for personal advantage; who has evinced more freedom from party bias and subserviency than any other leading public man in Upper Canada.' Although Sandfield's private life was clearly 'above suspicion,' an 'impartial man' he certainly was not. Like Robert Baldwin and Joseph

8 *Leader*, 12, 16, 18, 20 July 1867.
9 Macdonald Papers, Macdonald to Horan, 9 Aug. 1867, and *Leader*, 1 Aug. 1867.
10 Macdonald Papers, Macdonald to T. Colton, 9 Aug. 1867.
11 *Globe*, 3 and 7 Aug. 1867.

Howe, Sandfield Macdonald believed in using responsible government to reward the faithful. Even after he resigned the Ontario premiership, he was still calling himself a Reformer. Certainly he regarded the Brownites as the factious ones, factious from a Reform point of view, but he never joined Ryerson in denouncing party government as immoral. Nor did he ever adequately explain any permanent future position for the Coalition Reformers. In the election campaign he stressed his 'obstinate' leadership over the Ontario 'Combination.' He also emphasized the need to prevent Ontario from being politically isolated; it was important to 'harmonize' the two levels of government in the early days of the new system, one which still caused him many misgivings.[12]

The overwhelming majority of Ontarians thus endorsed Confederation and Sandfield's Patent Combination. They sent to the old red brick legislative building on Front Street about 50 members, out of a house of 82, who were prepared to follow the semi-invalid from Cornwall. But only 13 of the entire 82 had any previous parliamentary experience, and among the 50 supporters there were more Conservatives than Coalition Reformers.

Sandfield's ministers were all present for the opening of the first session of the legislature on 27 December 1867. Arriving in a coach and four and accompanied by a large military staff, Major General Stisted (whom Brown told his wife was 'an old fool'[13]) was greeted by two military bands, several companies of the Queen's Own, the Toronto Royals and a Grand Trunk Battalion. He received an eighteen-gun salute. The speech from the throne, which he read the next day, was a cautious document; the government planned to complete the structure of the provincial administration, promote local works, and encourage immigration and settlement through a liberal free land grant and homestead law. The speech also referred to the 'larger opportunities' available to Upper Canadians now that they had their own legislature and government.[14]

As the session progressed Sandfield told McDougall that he was 'jubilant' over the current state of politics.[15] The opposition, led by

12 *Ibid.*, 22, 25, 26, 28, 30 July and 7 and 8 Aug. 1867.
13 Brown Papers, Brown to Anne Brown, 16 Jan. 1868.
14 *Globe*, 29 Dec. 1867.
15 Macdonald Papers, McDougall to Macdonald, 15 Jan. 1868.

McKellar, seemed weak and unsure of itself, although Blake launched an almost successful attack on dual representation. Toronto that winter seemed gay and festive; again it was the seat of government with its own lieutenant governor. There was a fantastic round of balls and parties where attendance often crossed party lines. George Brown even had Sandfield and a few other coalitionists in for dinner. In such an environment, Sandfield thrived. On one occasion he had over sixty guests, including the lieutenant governor, entertained by a military band, but Brown, who was present, was unimpressed with the lavishness. During the session, the old tory backbencher, Sir Henry Smith, caused minor trouble by jamming the legislature with an over-abundance of private bills. Sandfield fought against this American tendency which outraged his notions of responsible government. He was also embarrassed by clashes in public between Wood and M. C. Cameron. But the passage of the Homestead Act, preliminary organization of the colonizing district of Muskoka, and provision for the northward extension of certain railways, more than offset this bickering. Sandfield's Homestead Act, obviously modelled by Richards on the American act of 1862, allowed the government to open for settlement surveyed crown lands which were not mineral or pine timber lands. After five years of free residence, the occupant would be granted title to one hundred acres. The government also provided that such grantees could purchase another one hundred acres at fifty cents an acre. Sandfield proudly informed Sir John that Ontario welcomed all classes of settlers willing to make the province their home, giving 'free grants with the most favourable Homestead Exemption Laws to be found on the Statute Books that we have read.'[16]

During the next three years, Sandfield had the legislature meet in the late fall and early winter for two or three months. Gradually the developmental policy of the Patent Combination unfolded. In the second session the Homestead Act was amended to increase the free grant to two hundred acres, and shortly thereafter a system of compensation for costs connected with drainage and land reclamation was established. Colonization roads were being extended northward. More and more developmental railways were charted; in early 1871 the legislature made available a fund of one and a half million dollars to be spent on aiding railroads, after construction was completed,

16 *Ibid.*, JSM to Macdonald, 5 June 1868.

that had pushed into the land grant areas of the province. Inland water transportation on the Muskoka Lakes was also encouraged. Late in 1868, to promote mining, Sandfield had all taxes and duties on minerals abolished, and the next year, to encourage immigration to Ontario, he had an informative pamphlet published and distributed widely in Britain. He also had appointed a special commissioner of emigration who would reside overseas.

Attorney General Sandfield did not neglect judicial and legislative reform. Over the objections of Sir John, he had the recorder's court and other outdated judicial bodies abolished and the jurisdiction of surviving courts redefined. One of Sandfield's few significant moves as a federal member came when he successfully secured parliamentary approval for a measure to ensure that persons arrested on criminal charges in Ontario and Quebec had the right to choose between trial at once without jury or trial by jury at the next assizes. His provincial Independence of Parliament Act in 1868 excluded members of the dominion cabinet and dominion and provincial civil service from membership in the Assembly. The Election Act of the same year attempted to eliminate some of the abuses evident in previous contests and to broaden the electorate. Elections would be on one day only and on the same day throughout the province. The property requirement was lowered and the multiple vote eliminated by requiring residence as well as ownership to qualify. The number of polling subdivisions significantly increased. But the master of Ivy Hall would not go all the way toward a male democracy. The franchise to him was clearly related to property. He regarded attempts to include adequate salary as an alternative to property in qualifying for the municipal vote as 'revolutionary'; men who had worked hard to acquire property had to be protected from such vagaries as 'bank clerks.'[17] Neither the secret ballot nor the elimination of dual representation was included in this reform, but A. A. Dorion congratulated his former associate on his progressive reform and on 'the true liberal spirit which pervades all your proceedings.'[18]

Under Sandfield, educational reform, stalled by Confederation politics, now proceeded. Because there was as yet no minister of education (despite Ryerson's urgings), Sandfield was closely involved

17 *Leader*, 25 Feb. 1868.
18 JSM Papers, Dorion to JSM, 11 Dec. 1868.

in the work of the chief superintendent. But the two men did not always see eye to eye. Like Baldwin, Sandfield had long agreed with the Grits that state aid to university education should be limited to the non-denominational University of Toronto. For years the legislature had also been authorizing annual grants to three denominational colleges, Queen's, Victoria and Regiopolis; by 1868 four more small institutions, all Catholic, were receiving aid, and still smaller ones were applying or about to apply. This was inefficient, costly and a violation of the principle of separation of church and state. Besides, the new institutions were anything but universities. In February 1868 Sandfield announced that state aid to all of these institutions would end in eighteen months. Immense pressure from Principal Snodgrass of Queen's and President Nelles of Victoria and from Sir John, all backed by Ryerson who believed in multidenominational support and in the inseparability of science and religion, was of no avail. Sandfield, backed by the opposition, held firm. The grants stopped, and provincial aid to denominational institutions has never recommenced. In the midst of this controversy, Sir John was anything but loyal to his colleague when he asserted to Principal Snodgrass that Sandfield's 'only claim to public support is his reputation for economy, and to keep that up he sacrifices every principle of justice' and that this line was already 'almost worn to rags.'[19]

Nevertheless, over Blake's vehement objections, Reformer Sandfield did support Ryerson's long-desired reorganization of the primary and secondary school system, a liberal reorganization which Ryerson had outlined in his report for 1868. It called for free schools at the primary and secondary level, compulsory attendance, standard qualifications for inspectors and teachers, municipal grants for grammar as well as elementary schools, superannuation for teachers and more science in the curriculum. Led by Blake, the opposition tried to destroy Ryerson who early in the second session tendered his resignation. But Sandfield, Cameron and a select committee backed the chief superintendent, who thereupon went on a circuit of the province explaining his proposed reforms and listening to replies. Ryerson was convinced, and he convinced Sandfield, that the province was ready for the change and that the Grits were on this issue reactionaries.

19 Macdonald Papers, 14 Dec. 1868.

Then, before the bill could be introduced, reform was almost lost when Ryerson clashed with Treasurer Wood. Ryerson disliked Wood's Grittism and his vehement opposition to aid to the colleges, despite the Methodist support he had obtained in the election. Now Wood, through his new centralized accounting system, was interfering with salaries in the education department. Ryerson was furious and wrote intemperate letters to Cameron imputing collusion between Wood and his erstwhile Brownite friends. Cameron, fearful of a public uproar, had to demand the withdrawal of the letters. Sandfield, annoyed and embarrassed at this violation of responsible government, wisely asserted that Ryerson should have complained directly to the premier. For over a month, Ryerson stubbornly refused to withdraw the letters. Finally, Sandfield had to take personal charge of the affair. He expressed his warmest friendship for Ryerson, through Ryerson's assistant, J. G. Hodgins, who, using this protestation, finally got Ryerson to concede. On 22 March 1869, after Ryerson's tour had been completed, the two old friends had a secret meeting and henceforth worked closely together to affect the educational reform.[20]

When Cameron introduced the education bill in late 1869, it was 'kicked and cuffed and hacked so unmercifully,'[21] that the premier, with Ryerson's approval, temporarily withdrew it. A modestly amended version was reintroduced in the next session, early in 1871, and Brown in the *Globe* and Blake in the legislature returned to the attack, with Sandfield expressing his confidence in the 'sagacity' of his chief superintendent. Blake condemned compulsory attendance as illiberal, useless and an encouragement to lawlessness. The enforced end of fees was arbitrary. In true Grittish fashion, he particularly attacked the centralizing nature of the reform. He also rejected the introduction of science, claiming it would undermine the 'practical branches,' the 'three R's.'[22] Nevertheless, the bill secured third reading on 14 February and thereby became the most progressive achievement of Sandfield's premiership.[23] The same year legislation was passed for the establishment of an Ontario Agricultural College and Farm, of a technical college (ultimately the Ryerson Institute of Technology) and for an expansion of the Toronto Normal School.

Sandfield also made 'extensive and important' advances in health

20 Sissons, *Ryerson*, II, 562–73.
21 *Globe*, 15 Dec. 1869.
22 *Ibid.*, 18, 25, 26 Jan. 1871.
23 Sissons, *Ryerson*, II, 564–87.

and social welfare.[24] Recognizing the limitations of private initiative, he again showed himself more progressive than his opponents. He rejected the social Darwinism preached by the *Globe*, which railed against 'promiscuous alms-giving' as a fatal promotion of pauperism among 'the worthless and the improvident.' Brown's organ argued that it was 'true mercy to say that it would be better that a few individuals die of starvation than that a pauper class should be raised up with thousands devoted to crime and the victims of misery.'[25] By contrast, Sandfield argued that sooner or later public charities would have to be supported by direct taxation.[26] Prisons were in crying need of reform. Early in 1868, Sandfield's Prison and Asylums Inspection Act provided for thorough annual inspection of all such public institutions by one paid inspector with power to order improvements. Under the act, Sandfield had the brilliant and dedicated J. W. Langmuir appointed. For fourteen years he steadily ameliorated prison conditions. Langmuir's area of authority was also broadened to include provincially supported hospitals when the debt-ridden Toronto hospital was reorganized and given provincial support. Urged on by Langmuir, the usually parsimonious premier channelled much of the provincial surplus toward institutions for the handicapped and toward penal reform. Sandfield pushed for the establishment of district prisons with attached farms to alleviate overcrowding in county jails and especially to promote rehabilitation. In 1871 construction began on a large central prison in Toronto. Before Confederation, the mentally ill who were not under family care or in inadequate institutions in Toronto, Kingston and Orillia, were treated in overcrowded prisons as common criminals. Now, as facilities were quickly made available, Sandfield had them transferred to asylums. For this purpose he leased and then obtained from the federal government Rockwood asylum in the Kingston area. He aso used two buildings at the University of Toronto until large additions could be made to the Toronto asylum. In 1870 a new asylum was built in London. Sandfield also arranged, on a fee basis from the federal government, to care for the criminally insane. By 1876 Langmuir considered On-

24 Richard B. Splane, *Social Welfare in Ontario: 1791–1893* (Toronto 1965), p. 11.
25 *Globe*, 24 Feb. 1874.
26 *Ibid.*, 3 and 31 Dec. 1868.

tario's treatment of its insane to be 'enlightened and humane.'[27] Sandfield also had constructed the Belleville Institute for the Deaf and Dumb and the Brantford Institute for the Blind, the latter not completed until 1872. He unfortunately failed, however, in his attempt to hold municipalities responsible for the care of the poor.

None of these social achievements seemed to capture the public mind. Sandfield was never able to free himself from the persistent Grit charge that he was a kept man, a prisoner of Sir John, and hence unfit to head the government of the strongest province in the new dominion. Like Sir John, Sandfield by conviction had a preference for legislative union. Nevertheless he accepted the quasi-federalism of the British North America Act. Sir John had professed privately the belief that within the lifetime of his generation, the provincial legislatures and governments would be absorbed in the 'General Power'[28]; he did not intend that the Canadian system be co-ordinate, classical or American federalism. The fathers had established subordinate federalism or 'legislative union with a constitutional recognition of the federal principle'[29]; the relationship between the general and provincial governments was intended to be more an imperial than a federal one. In 1868, Sir John emphasized that while disallowance by Whitehall was in rapid decline, disallowance by Ottawa was likely to continue to be used with considerable frequency to check provincial error and to promote the national interest, really the Canadian imperial interest.[30] This was the dispensation under which Sandfield operated.

In office Sandfield accepted the Macdonaldian system. The majoritarian Grits did not. Their grass roots went back to the localism, minus the radicalism, of William Lyon Mackenzie, of the original Clear Grits, and of George Sheppard. During the Confederation negotiations George Brown had been a centralist and a nationalist. Now he and his lieutenants embraced the deep decentralist sentiment of so many of their followers. Ontario liberalism in thus taking up provincial rights was sidetracked away from major reform. Toronto's

27 Splane, *Social Welfare*, p. 205.
28 Macdonald Papers, Macdonald to M. C. Cameron, 19 Dec. 1864.
29 *Gazette*, Montreal, 9 Sept. 1864.
30 W. E. Hodgins, *Correspondence, Reports of the Minister of Justice and Orders-in-Council upon the Subject of Provincial Legislation, 1867–84* (Ottawa 1888), p. 5.

evangelical, commercial and professional élite gave leadership to this liberalism; the aggressive but profoundly conservative farmers and townsfolk of the great peninsula gave liberalism its electoral strength. Both groups found the role of Montreal and the French fact too strong in the new Canada. Sir John was too susceptible to non-Ontario pressures. John Sandfield seemed too subservient to Sir John. Both groups wanted full provincial autonomy and co-ordinate federalism.

Sandfield was not a provincial rightist, but neither was he at all submissive. He was clearly his own master. How could he be anything else? Indeed, Sir John found him much too ambitious, cantankerous, and radical, a man who 'now paddles his own canoe.'[31] In 1868 the prime minister was considering entering the Ontario house to act as 'a check on the powers that be in Toronto.' By February 1871, so alarmed was he by 'radical' legislation, that he became convinced that Ontario needed an upper house.[32] In fact the premiership of Ontario and Sandfield's own personality led him into many quarrels, mostly private or 'quiet' ones, with his namesake.

Sandfield accepted Sir John's detailed perusal and criticism of provincial legislation; the exchanges of letters both public and private on this subject are rather extensive. Although Sir John had the governor general disallow only two Ontario statutes, he frequently urged Sandfield to amend or repeal certain laws. Sometimes Sandfield received this supervision with good grace; other times he fought back, and sometimes won.[33] But slowly, as a nation-building fervour faltered, the Grits seemed to convince more and more Ontarians that Sandfield was servile. Claiming to defend Confederation, they were really out to destroy the Macdonaldian system which they either rejected or never understood. Although the new system did not fully triumph until 1896, its first victim was John Sandfield Macdonald.

The personal relationships between the two Macdonalds had their ups and downs. In June of 1868, Sandfield was 'in bad humour' over Sir John's intention of appointing tired William Howland as lieuten-

31 Macdonald Papers, Macdonald to R. Stephenson, 8 Oct. 1867.

32 Joseph Pope, *Memoirs of the Rt. Hon. Sir John Alexander Macdonald GCB* (Ottawa *c.* 1894), II, 373; and Macdonald Papers, Macdonald to Macpherson, 7 Feb. 1871.

33 Numerous letters in the Macdonald and JSM Papers, and Hodgins, *Correspondence*.

ant governor of Ontario. It may be that Sandfield wanted the job himself, or simply to be consulted.[34] It was only after 'repeated refusals' that Sandfield agreed to accompany Sir John in his delicate late summer mission to Halifax, aimed at winning over Joseph Howe from repeal by offering Nova Scotia somewhat better financial terms. Sir John was convinced that Sandfield, being Ontario's Joseph Howe, could render 'Yeoman Service' to the Canadian cause by telling his 'great personal friend' that Ontario had not suffered from union. Sandfield not only relented, but, as Sir John suggested, he took along one of his vivacious daughters who was chaperoned by Lady Macdonald. Cartier and McDougall were also along, but it was Sandfield's presence which particularly attracted favourable attention in the Maritime press: his 'good social qualities' had always 'secured him hosts of friends,' and few Upper Canadians had been 'more courteous to the people of the Maritime Provinces.'[35] Hunting in pairs again proved successful. Howe relented. Returning to Toronto, Sandfield affably informed Sir John that he was reinvigorated by their 'late most agreeable trip.'[36]

Then in August 1869, after the ill-fated McDougall had been appointed lieutenant governor–elect of Rupert's Land, relations seriously deteriorated. Sir John was looking for a new senior 'Reformer' for his coalition; he also needed a new finance minister, one not tied to the Bank of Montreal. Francis Hincks, now Sir Francis, was back in the country. If there was one thing that John Sandfield and George Brown agreed on, it was that their old foe was no Reformer, that the return to politics of the railway profiteer and party betrayer was unwanted. Yet Sir John was lionizing Sir Francis and rumours were afoot. Sandfield refused to attend a banquet in Ingersoll in honour of the two great 'Reformers,' Sir Francis and himself. Sir Francis only perceived half the truth when he informed Sir John that Sandfield saw him as an interloper.[37] Nevertheless, that October Hincks was appointed minister of finance. Soon afterwards the prime minister was hearing rumours that the premier and certain disgruntled Con-

34 Macdonald Papers, Howland to Macdonald, 1 June 1868; PAC, McDougall Papers, 21 June 1868; and *Leader*, 5 June and 2 July 1868.
35 JSM Papers, Macdonald to JSM, 24 July 1868; *Leader*, 7 Aug. 1868; *Morning Chronicle* (Halifax), 14 Aug. 1868; and Pope, *Memoirs*, II, 28.
36 Macdonald Papers, 22 Aug. 1868.
37 *Ibid.*, Hincks to Macdonald, 20 Sept. 1869.

servatives were co-operating with George Brown to defeat Hincks in Renfrew North. Hincks won, but he complained of 'rebellion in the ranks' which had 'sprung from various causes but rely on it that Sandfield is at the bottom.'[38]

Hincks and Sandfield never established cordiality, but there seems to have been no confrontation over him between the two Macdonalds. The day before Hincks wrote his letter of accusation, Sandfield was informing the prime minister, in a matter-of-fact way, about the speedy and happy completion of the throne debate in Toronto. He was then secretly involved in a complicated argument with Sir John over the Ontario legislature's assertion of the right to supplement the salaries of certain federally appointed judgeships and to remove under certain circumstances county court judges. Agreeing to moderate the form, Sandfield held to the principle. Sir John thereupon wrote that he would have to disallow the supply act which contained the offensive provisions, but he did concede that if Ontario repassed the measures in separate bills moderated as Sandfield had now suggested, they would not be disallowed without orders from the Colonial Office. So even before the act was disallowed on 22 January 1870 Sandfield had the new bills passed. It was not easy to be an Ontario Reform premier of a coalition government, with a master politician as prime minister of Canada.

But in Ottawa Sir John had had his troubles, and these were now to involve Sandfield. Galt had left the cabinet in late 1867. In early 1868, Cartier in a friendly exchange of letters with Brown, had tried to persuade his old opponent to join with himself and Galt to overthrow Sir John. Richard Cartwright had deserted Sir John over Hincks' appointment. When in December 1869 McDougall was rebuffed on the Red River by Louis Riel and abandoned by Sir John, he returned to Ottawa and sat on the opposition benches with Galt. Now Cartwright and Galt planned a major coup which would have involved Cartier and Sandfield. Galt saw an interested Sandfield in Cornwall. In the end nothing came of the plot, but Brown must have heard of it. He sent a secret envoy to sound out Sandfield as to whether or not he was willing to become federal leader of a reorganized opposition. When the *Globe* denied these 'overtures,' the Cornwall *Freeholder*, on Sandfield's authority, confirmed them, noting

38 *Ibid.*, 8 Nov. 1869.

that the denial from an organ which had constantly abused the Patent Combination showed 'what an unreliable, unworthy and contemptible politician' Brown was.[39] Soon after there were further encounters with Hincks over federal-provincial finance and an alleged snubbing by Hincks and the Prime Minister; Premier Sandfield, 'sadly disturbed,' even went into the *Globe* office and complained bitterly for two hours to his enemy George Brown. 'Pitching into Hincks and John A,' he spoke 'guardingly of Cartier' and hinted that he foresaw a breakdown in the federal cabinet; he urged Brown to return to parliament and emphasized the need for a new 'strong Government,' founded on a 'national party' of the 'best men.'[40]

In the spring of 1870 it was probably too late for Brown to reconsider his stand even if Sandfield had been willing to move. Brown speculated that Sandfield did expect an imminent 'break up' and either wanted Alexander Mackenzie and the Grits available if he were called on to be prime minister or else wanted to be included if Mackenzie were called. Brown described Sandfield's approach as 'impudence'; he was certain that Donald A. knew nothing of it and that only Macpherson, Galt, King, and Brydges were his 'coadjutors' with an 'acknowledged sympathy from Cartier.' According to Brown, other Grits believed that the two chief ministers were 'thick as thieves' and that the contrary talk was all 'fudge.'[41] Galt had really tried, but he had failed. Sir John knew about the plot but was convinced that Sandfield would in the end remain 'sound and true,' largely because he could do nothing else safely.[42]

The Grits were concentrating their efforts on overthrowing Sandfield. The *Globe*, opposing Sandfield's 'dummy' role in the federal parliament, had castigated him for voting for financial grants to the Intercolonial Railway and for the 'better terms' for Nova Scotia.[43] In the Ontario legislature the brilliant Edward Blake had moved in November 1869 a series of thirteen resolutions condemning increased aid to Nova Scotia; the government defeated twelve of them, but on the thirteenth, calling for constitutional legislation to prevent the federal parliament from disturbing 'the financial relations established

39 *Leader*, 14 March 1870, quoting the *Freeholder* at length.
40 Mackenzie Papers, Brown to Mackenzie, 14 March 1870.
41 *Ibid.*, Brown to Mackenzie, 21 March 1870.
42 Pope, *Memoirs*, II, 72, Macdonald to John Rose, 23 Feb. 1870.
43 22 May and 5 June 1869.

by the Union Act,' ranks had been about to break. Sandfield thereupon had the government support the resolution.[44] Now in 1870 Blake had assumed the position of leader of the opposition. From neither Blake nor Brown would Sandfield get any mercy. In Ottawa in April 1870 Sandfield vainly voted against Sir John on the matter of renewing and extending the charter of the Canada Central Railway, not only westward from Sand Point along the Ottawa valley, but from Ottawa down on the Quebec side to Montreal, thus making it what it ultimately became, a vital link in a future Pacific railroad. The Canada Central and its associate line, the Brockville to Ottawa, were the railroads in which R. W. Scott was concerned; the eastern extension involved other foes of the premier's. The *Globe* said that Sandfield's vote was merely 'senseless opposition,' and related to old grievances and not to Ontario interests.[45] On 21 December 1870 the *Globe* made perhaps its most insulting personal attack on the premier:

Petulance, bad temper, a garrulous, half-wandering incoherent style of speech, a littleness and total want of dignity of bearing and expression; a shabby, shuffling way of wandering out of it; a reckless style of assertion and a strange forgetfulness today of what may have been the utterance of yesterday; this, without the least exaggeration is a fair description of Mr. Sandfield Macdonald as the head of the Government and leader of the Legislative Assembly of Ontario. The question that a stranger instinctively asks himself is, by what strange freak of fortune this queer caricature of a practical statesman has been elevated to a prominent position in the politics of his country.

Rumours of federal reorganization had continued. After the passage in May 1870 of the Manitoba Act and the dispatch of the military expedition to the Red River, the prime minister had fallen seriously ill with gall stones. Few thought he would recover let alone be able to resume his duties. Many in the Montreal business community wanted John Sandfield as successor. Cartier was too French; Hincks was anathema in that city. Galt was brilliant but too extravagant and too republican. As Horace Forbes, one member of the community, expressed it, Sandfield was the man; under him Ontario was 'well managed' with 'strict economy' in every department, while with

44 *Globe* and *Leader*, 24 Nov. 1869.
45 *Globe*, 28 April 1870.

'great liberality and personal integrity' he promoted general prosperity. Especially laudable were his land and immigration policies and his educational reforms. Sandfield's one flaw, Forbes wrote, was that unlike Sir John he had not always the command of his temper and often 'sneered down opponents,' men who did 'not mind a hard hit,' but could not bear a sneer. Still Sandfield was 'clear headed' and able to deal with Canada's expanding external commercial relations as well as internal development. Forbes urged Sandfield to purchase the Montreal *Gazette* as a vital step toward the prime ministership.[46]

The Grits knew none of this. They were busy attacking the premier for alleged abuse of patronage. Like Baldwin, he frankly believed in patronage. But his lack of finesse got him into trouble. During the election he had jokingly told an audience in Hamilton that they might shortly 'have some axes to grind' and that if they were not 'now disposed to lend a helping hand ... they could not blame anyone but themselves if they found themselves cut off from public support.'[47] The Hamiltonians ignored the hint, and Hamilton did not get the large asylum it had wanted. The *Globe* claimed that the system of the 'axe grinder' was legalized bribery.[48] During the second session when nine Reform members of the legislature publicly announced their refusal to submit to dictation from Brown, the *Globe* dubbed them the 'Nine Martyrs' and accused them of having their price, known to every member.[49] Given the moral effectiveness of the opposition organs and the bluntness of Sandfield's operation of the recognized system, the premier seemed incapable of turning patronage to advantage. Besides, Sandfield hardly regarded the Ontario legislature as a sovereign parliament; in contrast to his approach in the old Canadian legislature, he now emphasized the role of the provincial executive. Criticized more for his parsimony than for his extravagance, he insisted, despite condemnation, in having the house vote huge undifferentiated sums for each department; he also refused to have his auditor made directly responsible to the house. When in 1871 the legislature allocated one and a half million dollars from the provincial surplus to promote new railways, the disposition of the money was left to the cabinet, led by a man who had earlier stated that it was his principle that 'if the Government had anything to give, they would

46 JSM Papers, 17 June 1870.
47 *Globe*, 7 Sept. 1867.
48 *Ibid.*, 14 April 1869.
49 *Ibid.*, 20 Jan. 1869.

give it to their friends, and if they had anything to give after that, they would give it to their opponents.'[50] In 1871 the *Globe* claimed that this was much too large an amount to entrust to any government, especially just before an election.[51] Yet the power was not abused. Sandfield himself claimed that half his problem was his 'bad habit of joking with a grave face,' that he could hardly 'make a jovial remark in the lobbies or in the halls of a hotel without there being some spies around to tell it; and the next day it would appear in the *Globe* with the worst possible construction put upon it.'[52] Yet half a year after this confession, Sandfield is said to have remarked to a delegation from Grittish Strathroy wanting a registry office located in their town, 'What the hell has Strathroy done for me?'[53]

For the premier, these were personally ambivalent years. Sometimes he seemed exhilarated; other times, particularly as his health faltered more and more frequently, he seemed to want to be rid of it all. Louise often acted as her father's corresponding secretary in Toronto, but Christine and most of the family generally remained in Cornwall, and he grew tired of travelling across the province and up to Ottawa. Late in 1868 he had complained to Lord Monck of the 'weight of official obligation,' asserting that he was 'anxious to get rid of the life I have been leading for nearly eight and twenty years.'[54] Yet in his friendly relations with that governor general he had found one of the joys of the past few years. Monck, backing Sir John's view of the role of lieutenant governors, had exulted in Sandfield's appointment and final attachment to coalition.[55] Now in 1868, as he was leaving Canada, Monck wished Sandfield in a personal letter 'all prosperity and happiness – political and personal.' Urging him 'to find me out' soon in Britain, he wrote that he hardly needed to 'indulge in any professions of personal regard toward you now.' Sandfield thereupon reciprocated with a personal note which for him was untypically warm and affectionate. It would give him 'unspeakable pleasure to shake your hand and to bid you farewell,' he wrote; he hoped to be able soon 'to visit you across the sea.'[56]

But that was not to be so. Politics and his health kept him tied

50 *Ibid.*, 14 Jan. 1868.
51 *Ibid.*, 8 Feb. 1871.
52 *Leader*, 7 Jan. 1871.
53 *Globe*, 24 Aug. 1871.
54 JSM Papers, 12 Nov. 1868.
55 Macdonald Papers, Monck to Macdonald, 13 July 1867.
56 JSM Papers, Monck to JSM, 3 Nov. 1868 and JSM to Monck, 12 Nov. 1868.

down. All he could afford during that winter of 1868–69 was a brief working vacation to New York and Washington with Josephine. He returned with another 'infernal cold.'[57] If only his Reform colleagues in the cabinet were more loyal and competent. The Grittish Wood frequently disagreed openly with his colleagues and voted against Sandfield in Ottawa. Richards was less than adequate in crown lands, and even the *Leader* frequently called for his resignation.[58] Conservative Cameron, once he settled into the job, was more dependable. Still it was comforting to receive kind words from his old mentor, former Chief Justice W. H. Draper, who as the 'chill shadows of the evening of life' were fast descending on him voiced deepest appreciation for the way Sandfield had personally intervened to see that semi-retired judges benefited from salary increases.[59]

Late in 1869 he was again particularly ill. At times M. C. Cameron had to act as house leader. Around Christmas, he went down to Cornwall for several weeks of complete rest. He returned late in January 'much improved' and ready for a round of legislative and social events.[60] On 10 February 1870 he was back home where 'the favoured son' of Cornwall was ushered through the crowded streets to be honoured at a mass dinner given by his constituents in the Town Hall, lavishly decorated for the occasion. Over 700 guests, including many of the leading men of Toronto and Montreal besides the 'elite and fashion of Cornwall,' crowded into the Hall to pay tribute to the veteran parliamentarian.[61] Later that month he attended in Ottawa the great ball in honour of the visit of Prince Arthur, the queen's son, who opened the federal parliament. In plain evening dress, the premier could be distinguished on the dance floor by 'an unusually immense collar even for him, in which he seemed to take considerable pride, although it was worn at the risk of momentarily lopping his ears off.' Undaunted by fear of such an accident he danced 'with a great deal of industry, hardly missing a quadrille in the first two hours.'[62]

The most important festive event took place on 1 March, 1870, with the double wedding of two of the Sandfield daughters: Josephine

57 PAC, microfilm of the Lennox and Addington Historical Collections, John Stevenson Papers, JSM to Stevenson, 4 March 1869.
58 20 Sept. and 6 Nov. 1869.
59 JSM Papers, 26 Jan. 1869.
60 *Leader*, 18 Jan. 1870.
61 *Ibid.*, 11 Feb. 1870.
62 *Ibid.*, 26 Feb. 1870.

to Jean Langlois, LLD, QC, former professor of law at Laval and now member of parliament for Montmorency, and Louise to Lieutenant J. G. Uppleby of the Royal Artillery. Witnessed by many of the political and financial élite of Ontario and Quebec, John Sandfield gave away his two lovely daughters, in white satin gowns and tulle veils, attended by four bridesmaids in billowy dresses of white tarlatan which contrasted with the sashes of the Macdonald tartan they wore around their waists.[63] Following the ceremony in Ivy Hall an exhausting *déjeuner* was served. With Cartier looking on, Sir John A. Macdonald proposed the toast to the brides to which Langlois replied in French and Uppleby in English. Leaving by special train, the Langlois honeymooned for several weeks in New England, the Upplebys for several months in the southern states. In Washington the Upplebys were received by President Grant and invited to a party at the White House. Louise mentioned that she had never before felt so thankful to her parents for making her study French as well as English, because many of the ambassadors at the President's party spoke French. Prince Arthur too was in attendance. Typically awkward, Sandfield had told Ryerson before the wedding that 'these things would happen' and that Ryerson's daughter, Sophie, who was Louise's closest friend, probably 'knew more about it than he did.' Yet he 'laughed very heartily' when he told of a Peterborough man who had written to compliment the premier on his policy of public economy which he believed was 'so well illustrated in his personal example as to make one *déjeuner* do for two marriages.'[64]

This awkwardness about the family never showed itself more clearly than the September of 1870 on his thirtieth wedding anniversary. His governmental responsibilities prevented him from being with Christine in Cornwall, so he wrote to her that it was 'fitting' that he should 'at least record' his conviction that he possessed a wife who had 'commended herself as worthy of more appreciation of her excellent qualities' than he with his 'peculiarities of temper' had shown. Despite his confessed shortcomings, he took 'great pride' in her 'varied accomplishments' and 'other qualities' which had earned her

63 *Ibid.*, 5 March 1870.

64 Sissons, *My Dearest Sophie*, pp. 181 and 186–87, Ryerson to Sophie, 8 Feb. and 18 May 1870.

the high regard of those who knew her. He closed with the expression of the 'fervent hope' that she might long enjoy health and have 'reason to be content' with her lot.[65] The man with whom Christine had eloped could harangue a crowd, administer and reform a province, deal out patronage, dance in quadrilles for two hours, and enjoy the gaieties of champagne, but he could not mention love to his wife.

He was off immediately for a tour of Muskoka, in 'the free land grant districts,' with Carling, Richards, several backbenchers, and English emigration promoters. The mode of travel was as uneven as the land he was opening: to Belle Ewart on Lake Simcoe by rail, along that lake and Lake Couchiching by steamer, from Washago through the granite of the Canadian Shield to Gravenhurst by stage, and from Gravenhurst to Bracebridge and the other ports on the lakes by the steamer *Wenonah* owned by the local coalition Reform MP, A. P. Cockburn. At prosperous but tiny Bracebridge, the villagers lit huge bonfires in honour of their premier and entertained him royally. In return, he spoke of the deep commitment of his government, a 'Government of the people not of party,' to northern development. Between Lakes Rosseau and Joseph, where men were completing the clearing of the river, the party pitched their tents. After vast quantities of food and the singing of patriotic songs by the politicians and camp songs by the woodsmen, the visitors retired. In the middle of the night tent-mates of the premier were suddenly aroused by a 'wild cry of alarm.' 'At the tent door loomed the spectral figure of the Attorney-General, dark against the glowing light of the camp fire, with extended arms and wild gestures. The cry of fire died on his lips. "I thought I was in a home of flames," he said penitently, and crept quietly back.' In the morning one of the Englishmen, Charles Marshall, nailed a pine plank to a tree, and 'inscribed on it the name newly decided on for the place,' while another, an Anglican priest, proclaimed it 'in the name of her Majesty Queen Victoria and of the Dominion of Canada, Port Sandfield.' Port Sandfield thus joined Port Carling and the townships of Wood and Stisted in linking the first Ontario government permanently to the nomenclature of Muskoka. On the tour the premier spoke to settlers in English and Gaelic, and at a house-building 'bee,' he demonstrated that he was 'an old

65 JSM Papers, 4 Sept. 1870.

hand' with the axe. The visitors were deeply impressed with the beauty of the waterways. The lakes had a glorious future.[66]

Yet many of the pioneers Sandfield was trying to settle on the rugged land south and east of the lakes, land not best suited for agriculture, were destined to become permanent recruits for the rural poor. The premier was not unaware of potential trouble. Committed to the North and happy with the success in the 'Muskoka territory,' he had earlier hinted in parliament, and had repeated emphatically in correspondence with the prime minister, that Ontario had 'now but indifferent lands to tempt the Emigrant,' that free lands would help to overcome the difficulty but that only a 'certainty of public works' to promote employment would keep the immigrant in Ontario.[67]

In the fall of 1870, with his health holding surprisingly firm, Sandfield seemed in great spirits. He personally took on the fall assizes in Hamilton, jokingly remarking in his first letter to the prime minister in ten months that this obviously indicated his courage in light of 'my axe grinding speech there in 1867.'[68] He mischievously had a 'new shirt collar of formidable dimensions made for the opening of the session' on 4 December.[69] The opening was graced by the prime minister and Lady Macdonald. Relations between the two chief ministers were again satisfactory. That same week, Josephine presented Sandfield with a grandson, who was named Eugene after Christine's brother.

In 1871 Sandfield had little time for grandchildren. The session which witnessed the passage of the education bill was a stormy one. The angry Grits were clearly on a militant election footing. Sir John, who saw the federal and provincial battles as one, counselled caution to Sandfield, suggesting an autumn election after a summer when the coalition could hold meetings all over the province to out-talk the Grits. Urging Sandfield to use the railway money to political effect, he promised tangible support stopping just short of causing a reaction.

66 Charles Marshall, *The Canadian Dominion* (London 1871), pp. 49–69; Thomas MacMurray, *Free Grant Lands of Canada* (Bracebridge 1871), pp. 82–85; Florence B. Murray, *Muskoka and Haliburton: 1615–1875: A Collection of Documents* (Toronto 1963), pp. xcix–cix, 341–43 and 402–6.
67 Macdonald Papers, 5 June 1868.
68 *Ibid.*, 29 Oct. 1870.
69 *Leader*, 30 Nov. 1870.

But by February Sandfield was convinced that he could not wait until the fall and that the best defence was a sudden spring offensive. The education bill had aroused some of the Catholics, who objected with Blake to compulsory attendance. Blake and Brown, aided by David Mills, MP, were trying desperately to woo the Irish Catholic vote. Brown now claimed that it had been his opponents who had really fought for 'Protestant dominancy.'[70] Several of the Catholic leaders, especially the brilliant criminal lawyer Hugh MacMahon of London, were urging their followers to desert the Macdonalds. MacMahon joined in the organization of a Catholic League aimed at securing more patronage for Catholics and more direct participation by Catholics in politics. Sandfield and MacMahon had a stormy confrontation in the director's car of the Great Western Railway, while Sandfield with Carling and Langmuir were on their way to inspect the London asylum. At the premier's request, Carling persuaded MacMahon, a regular passenger on the train, to come into the special car and there Sandfield lit into him 'with asperity.' MacMahon replied 'in kind,' emphasizing unkept promises of patronage for Catholics. Tempers got hotter and hotter, as MacMahon reviewed Sandfield's treatment of McGee and as Sandfield emphasized the popularity of his government throughout the province. In the end Sandfield accused MacMahon of being a 'Grit.' 'There is no means,' wrote MacMahon, 'of conveying the intense scorn with which he uttered this.' To Sandfield this was 'one of the most contemptuous epithets which could be applied to anyone.' MacMahon denied that he could ever be a genuine Grit: he was what Sandfield 'pretended to be – a Baldwin Reformer – and that was why he had supported him in the previous election.' In the election which followed, MacMahon worked hard to defeat the government. He had been warned that Sir John was about to receive an imperial appointment and that if Sandfield could carry the day in Ontario he would be in a position to assume the national leadership of the Conservative party, although Hincks and others would refuse to serve under him.[71] In an open letter, Brown urged the Catholic League to join with the Grits to form a 'reunion of the old Reform Party' of Robert Baldwin.[72] To

70 *Ibid.*, 8 Dec. 1870.
71 PAC, J. J. Murphy Papers, 'Reminiscences of Mr. Justice MacMahon.'
72 *Globe*, 9 March 1871.

Sandfield, Brown and the Grits were the antithesis of the Baldwinites, and it enraged him to hear his enemies misappropriate the term. He was the successor of Robert Baldwin, and he would win the election.

But more important than the imminent defection of a large part of the Catholic vote, Sandfield was suffering increasingly from the accusation of servility to Sir John. On 2 February 1871 Blake and McKellar had introduced a motion condemning the 'cold blooded murder' on the Red River of Thomas Scott by Louis Riel and charging the federal authorities with lack of zeal in prosecuting the matter. M. C. Cameron, for the government, successfully countered with an amendment which, deploring Scott's death and Riel's escape, noted current efforts by Manitoba to capture the fugitives and the inadvisability of Ontario interference in federal affairs.[73] Ironically, although the *Globe* had described Riel as merely the 'tool' of Bishop Taché, 'the real ruler of the Territory,'[74] Blake was so intent on winning the Catholic vote that he was exonerating the French Canadians from any role in the Red River troubles. In late February the house was prorogued and dissolved. The Cameron amendment was used again and again in the election to indicate Sandfield's docility to Sir John and hence, despite Blake's idiosyncrasies, to 'French domination at Fort Garry' and by extension throughout Canada.[75]

The ensuing campaign was short and heavy. Sandfield stood on his progressive record as the 'people's party' against the 'Factionists.'[76] He was accused at one and the same time of subservience, executive dictation, 'axe-grinding,' prodigality relative to northern development, and parsimony concerning the huge provincial surplus.[77] The *Globe* called on God to 'defend the right,' and Blake appealed to 'the intelligent judgment' of the people, and 'to Him in whom we live and move and have our being' in this hour of crisis in 'our national existence.'[78] The merciless *Globe* claimed that the ill Sandfield took a 'diseased pleasure in ostentatiously parading his utter personal want

73 *Leader*, 3 Feb. 1871.
74 23 April 1871.
75 *Leader*, 3 Feb. 1871 and *Globe*, 14 March 1871.
76 *Leader*, 27 Feb. 1871.
77 *Globe*, 15, 27 Feb. and 1, 2, 9, 10, 13, 14, 20 March 1870; *Mail* (Toronto), 3 June 1872.
78 Adam Shortt and Arthur Doughty, ed., *Canada and its Provinces*, XVII, *The Province of Ontario* (Toronto 1914), pp. 120–21.

of principle, and his scepticism of anything among all classes higher as a motive than self-interest in the coarsest and commonest sense of the term.'[79] Sir John, who had finally accepted Sandfield's analysis of the need for an early vote, regretted that the federal parliament was in session and that he personally had to leave the country for the negotiations in the American capital which would lead to the Treaty of Washington. He thought that he could help 'as well from Washington as from Ottawa' and that he would be back before the voting.[80] On both counts he was wrong. Negotiations in Washington went on beyond the election and soon were taxing all his energies. Worst of all Sandfield was ill with 'an infernal attack' of high fever when he called the election; he missed the opening of the federal parliament, made an appearance in Ottawa after recovering slightly, and then began campaigning in Ontario only to be forced to bed in Cornwall. Laid up for a fortnight with acute rheumatic pain and a sick stomach, he did not even get up 'with the aid of servants' until three days after the election. From his bed he dictated the vast numbers of letters necessary to co-ordinate an election, but he admitted later that the illness had produced an 'indifference about outside matters,' and had probably cost the government several seats.[81]

When the results were in, the shocked Sandfield made no attempt to disguise that the coalition vote had fallen severely. Nevertheless, rejecting the *Globe*'s claim that he had been thoroughly defeated, he was convinced that he could survive with a small 'working majority.'[82] With a few surprising exceptions, eastern Ontario had held; southwestern Ontario, especially around London but excluding Carling's seat, had gone overwhelmingly to the Grits. Within the coalition, the Conservative vote had declined, as the Catholics as well as the Orangemen 'had not been as true to their party as they formerly were wont to be.'[83] Although returned in Cornwall by acclamation, John Sandfield's hold locally was slipping. Two years earlier he had lost

79 13 March 1871.
80 JSM Papers, 24 and 26 Feb. 1871.
81 Macdonald Papers, JSM to Macdonald, 21 Feb. and 24 March 1871; also the *Mail*, 3 June 1872, and University of Toronto Library, Rare Books and Special Collections, William Tyrrell Papers, JSM to William Tyrrell, 9 and 26 Feb. and 29 March 1871.
82 Stevenson Papers, JSM to Stevenson, 24 March 1871; also Tyrrell Papers, 29 March 1871.
83 Macdonald Papers, JSM to Macdonald, 24 March 1871.

control of the town council. Since 1866 the town had had as mayor Dr. W. C. Allen, who opposed Sandfield. In 1871 it was to elect Angus Bethune, a staunch Grit. James Craig in Glengarry beat back a serious challenge; William Colquhoun, Sandfield's man in Stormont, won by such a small margin (five votes) that his Grit opponent, James Bethune, immediately instituted controverted election proceedings. James, Angus's son, was backed almost openly by Sandfield's brother Donald; personal and business relations between the brothers remained tolerable but Donald's open identification with the Reform opposition federally and his warm friendship with Mackenzie and Brown was a great embarrassment.[84]

For the rest of the spring, the premier remained ill in Cornwall and then at the mineral baths in St Catharines. Rumour was that he would resign before the new legislature met. The proud Scot, who had lost none of his fighting spirit, denied the talk, vowing that he would 'meet the House, if spared to that time, even if I have to be carried there in a blanket and confront all assailants face to face.'[85] But it was the end of June before he could return to his duties in Toronto, and even then he looked seriously ill. The *Globe* and Blake kept up the attack, and many Conservatives were restless; Sir John had to intervene to ease the pressure on Sandfield. In July, when he was temporarily in better health, Sandfield strengthened his team by switching around Cameron and Richards, thus bringing a little more energy into the sensitive crown lands office. Perhaps he also knew of the scandal made public in August: with Richards' knowledge, surveyors in Muskoka and Haliburton had been supplementing their salaries by obliging employees to sign for more money than they received.

The mood of expectancy was at its peak when the legislature finally met on 7 December 1871. Eight seats were technically vacant, six because of charges of electoral irregularities under the Controverted Elections Act of 1871. The members could not take their seats until the appeals had been heard in the courts. Taking appeals out of committees of the house had been a great reform, but it was now used by the Grits to destroy Sandfield. Sandfield was convinced that

84 William Colquhoun Papers, in the possession of Mrs. W. H. McNairn, Dundas, JSM to William Colquhoun, 31 Aug. 1871.
85 *Leader*, 24 May 1871.

he could not fairly be overthrown while so many seats were vacant. Presumably in an attempt to silence the increasingly restless R. W. Scott, the premier had him elected as speaker. But the Opposition was in no mood for patience. Blake moved an amendment to the Address denouncing executive control over the railway fund. A government backbencher, on Sandfield's initiative, moved that Blake's amendment be postponed until all seats were filled; this was defeated by a majority of eight. Wood then attempted to soften the Blake amendment by a motion urging caution in the distribution of the fund, though still leaving it in the government's hands. When this failed, the Blake amendment carried by a vote of 40 to 33. The government had now been defeated on three votes; yet, to the opposition's fury, the premier refused to resign. He rose in his seat the next day, 15 December, to defend his staying in power: neither a defeat on an ordinary vote nor on a want of confidence motion, he stated, would induce the government to resign until all members were in their seats. Meanwhile, the government would carry out only its administrative duties and would not touch the fund.

On this same day E. B. Wood, while speaking in defence of the government's stand, resigned and two days later went over to the opposition. Collusion with Blake seemed certain. Sandfield now attempted to propose a sub-amendment to Alexander Mackenzie's want of confidence motion which had been affixed to Blake's old amendment. The speaker ruled the motion out of order. The want of confidence motion was then put and the government defeated by a majority of one – 37 to 36. The address-in-reply, which included Blake's and Mackenzie's motions, then passed 64 to 6. The government, in fact, had voted want of confidence in itself. Still the Premier refused to step down, merely saying that he would explain his stand later.

When the legislature assembled again on 18 December, Lieutenant-Governor Howland appeared, to read the reply and to announce that he would give consideration to any bill either repealing or amending the railway fund legislation. Still there was no mention of the government's resignation. The opposition objected vehemently and Blake moved an address to the lieutenant-governor giving the opinion that the continuation of the government in office was against the spirit of the constitution. Sandfield tried once again to defer debate on the issue, by moving the adjournment of the Assembly until February, but he was defeated by a majority of seventeen. Blake's motion was then put, and passed 44 to 25.

The Premier could now see no way out. At the opening of the next day's sitting, he rose to announce the resignation of his government. He defended his previous reluctance to resign, despite the series of defeats, and reminded the house that the railway fund had been approved 'by the largest majority that the Government has ever had.' Yet the opposition had 'enflamed the public mind and spread abroad the notion that the Executive had obtained extraordinary powers' in the distribution of the fund; as a result, many members had returned pledged to oppose the government. The government had lost the vote of confidence by only one vote when many seats were vacant; thus the premier believed that the vote was 'not decisive' and had stayed on from a sense of duty. Now the situation had changed and ministers were tendering their resignations. After denying charges of corruption and bribery and defending the idea of coalition, the veteran politician concluded by thanking his supporters and apologizing to anyone in the opposition whom he might have offended:

... if in the course of debate, I may have said anything offensive to any gentleman opposite, I hope my hon. friends on the other side will accept this apology from me. If I had said anything to wound the feelings of any gentleman, I did not intend it; and if any gentleman opposite said hard things of me, I am ready to forgive him, as I hope they are ready to forgive me.[86]

On 20 December, Edward Blake formed a government including Mackenzie and McKellar. It was rumoured that Blake offered Donald A. the provincial treasurership. Blake, who had always opposed coalition, announced the next day that R. W. Scott, until then speaker, would join the cabinet as commissioner of crown lands. The former premier, meanwhile, was busy moving out of his office and writing letters of explanation to his friends. To him the government's fall was the work of Scott. 'The Speaker,' he wrote Sir John, 'turned turtle on us.' It was perhaps because of this Conservative defection that Sandfield repeatedly told certain leading Conservatives who wanted him to attend a meeting after the defeat that he was off

86 *Globe*, 20 Dec. 1871.

to Cornwall and that they could all go to a much warmer climate, for all he cared. Scott, for his part, blamed the fall on Sandfield's 'utter want of tact,' his 'very bad management' in allowing the 'doubtful men ... to drift away,' and his 'hostility to Ottawa interests.' But Carling was convinced that Scott had successfully used all his influence to persuade more than half a dozen members to desert Sandfield in the final vote as a revenge for his refusal to support the interests of the Canada Central and the powerful timber barons allied to it.[87]

Sir John, who had the bad habit of deriding Sandfield behind his back, argued that Sandfield had had the 'game in his own hands' but had thrown it away when he lacked 'the pluck' to use the surplus to great political advantage and neglected to increase patronage by adding two new positions to the cabinet.[88] Yet seven months later in the federal election, Sir John almost fell from power when he himself decisively lost Ontario 38 seats to 50. Sandfield's criticism of the propriety of Blake's amendment had some validity. Before the legislature reassembled in mid-January, the coalition had won four of the five seats challenged by the Grits plus the one which it had challenged. Sandfield's one defeat was in Stormont, where James Bethune, boldly backed by Donald, was declared the winner. A few months earlier Donald had finally secured a federal charter to construct his long-dreamed-of railway, which in 1879 became known as the Canada Atlantic and of which he was the president, to run from Ottawa through his Alexandria to the St. Lawrence at Coteau Landing; to help Bethune, Donald had promised that the line would arc through northern Stormont.[89]

Sandfield was late in returning to his new seat to the left of the new speaker. M. C. Cameron was acting leader of the opposition and continued to be so even after the return of the former premier. In early February, Sandfield left his legislative duties to go to Montreal to sell shares for the Toronto *Mail*, a major newspaper which Sir John and others had designed in the fall to act as the main organ of the two coalition governments; it was to replace the inadequate

87 Macdonald Papers, JSM to Macdonald, 19 Dec. 1871; Scott Papers, Scott to Macdonald, 15 and 20 Dec. 1871, and Carling to Macdonald, 21 Dec. 1871.

88 Macdonald Papers, Macdonald to Carling, 23 Dec. 1871.

89 Mackenzie Papers, DAM to Mackenzie, 6 Feb. 1872.

Leader and *Telegraph* and to go for 'a National policy in Tariff matters.'[90] Initial plans had faltered, but now with Sandfield's intervention his good friend T. C. Patteson was to act as managing editor of the paper. It published its first issue on 13 March, and on 3 June it declared that John Sandfield, who was enthusiastic about 'protection as against free trade,' had really taken 'the leading part' in its establishment.

Back in the legislature by late February, Sandfield again defended his railway policy against charges of corruption. In March he was confined to his bed at Ivy Hall suffering from a severe cold. 'I secretly think,' he confided to Patteson, 'I have a touch of the horse distemper.'[91] In May he attended a few sittings of the house of commons and then saw two doctors, one in Cornwall and one in Montreal. Both told him that his heart was so 'displaced and impaired' from past illnesses that there was no hope of recovery.[92] He took the news philosophically, remarking to the Montreal doctor that in his thirty-two years of politics he had personally carried nothing away 'but a bag of old bones'; the doctor replied that that was better than 'a coffin full of gold, made by acts of corruption.'[93]

90 Macdonald Papers, Macdonald to T. C. Patteson, 24 Feb. 1872.
91 PAO, Patteson Papers, JSM to Patteson, 21 March 1872.
92 *Mail*, 3 and 10 June 1872.
93 Sissons, *My Dearest Sophie*, p. 225, Ryerson to Sophie, 16 June 1872.

7

'Upright and Zealous'

On Saturday, 1 June 1872, at 2.00 PM, at fifty-nine years of age, John Sandfield Macdonald died peacefully at Ivy Hall, surrounded by Christine, his brothers Donald and Alexander, and other members of the family. Much to Christine's gratification he died 'courageously' and 'a good Catholic.' After receiving the last rites of the church, he told Christine 'I am satisfied now that I have settled my religious affairs and my will.'[1] His 'thoughts clear and collected to the end,' Sandfield then reminded his family that his old Montreal friends, including George Stephen, Sir Hugh Allan, and E. H. King, were expected in town that day to see about the new plant of the Canadian Cotton Manufacturing Company which was about to go into production in Cornwall; they 'must be invited to luncheon.'[2]

The next day news of Sandfield's death spread throughout the province. A telegram was sent to the House of Commons and was received by the speaker just as Edward Blake was railing against the pocket borough of Cornwall. The funeral held on 4 June was probably the largest ever seen in Cornwall. Several thousand people, some of whom had come from Ottawa on a special train arranged by C. J. Brydges, streamed into the town to pay their last respects to the veteran politician and lawyer whose body was now laid out in the large dining room of Ivy Hall. Soon after noon, a procession of about

1 JSM Papers, Christine Macdonald to Josephine Langlois, 7 June 1872, and Langlois Papers, Jean Langlois to Josephine Langlois, 11 June 1872.
2 *Mail*, 3 June 1872.

2,000 vehicles and 'an immense throng of foot people' slowly made its way along the canal and through the principal street of the town north to St Andrews. There he was buried in the full dress of a queen's counsel, with a crucifix on his breast and a cross of white flowers at his head. The train with the dignitaries returned to Ottawa that same day for the evening sitting; John Sandfield had successfully moved the abolition of the adjournment of the Commons on the death of a member, and his own death had been the first since the new rule.[3]

In obituary tributes to Sandfield, the *Globe* and the London *Advertiser* somewhat invalidated the invective which they had formerly hurled against their opponent. The *Globe* pointed out that in 1854 Sandfield had been condemned to an early death, yet he had laboured on for eighteen more years with a 'hopeful, cheerful spirit,' and that 'perhaps the most special characteristic of Mr. Macdonald's mind was his personal independence.'[4] Yet throughout his premiership the paper had charged that he was a mere 'puppet' and 'dummy.' The *Advertiser*, which had called Sandfield 'a passive politician who glides along with his party to the right or to the wrong,' a traitor to the Reform cause, and a man who was 'nothing, if not mean,' now regarded his death 'as a political loss.' 'His past services in the cause of Liberalism and freedom of our political institutions, entitle him to a niche in the memory of the people.'[5] At the crossroads of St Andrews, a large monument, erected by friends from across the country, stands atop his grave. With slight but excusable excess, it proclaims the resting place of a man 'upright and zealous in the discharge of his public duties,' and infused with 'personal integrity' in his private life.

The man was gone, but the enigma remained. It was even in evidence in the will covering an estate of over $200,000.[6] His quiet brother Alexander and his partner Donald Ban MacLennan were executors with power to sell most of the real estate, including Ivy Hall. A residence and a rather generous annual stipend from the income

3 *Ibid.*, 3 and 5 June 1872.
4 3 June 1872.
5 27 March 1869, 19 Dec. 1871, and 3 June 1872.
6 JSM Papers.

of the estate were assigned to Christine, who lived in Cornwall until her death in 1909. Similar stipends went to the girls. Young 'Georgie' Sandfield, a student at Upper Canada College, was to receive support for his education, and if diligent he was to be treated like the girls. But Henry Sandfield was almost cut off. After a brilliant record at Rugby, he had just entered his father's firm. He was granted without right of sale a rural lot near St Raphael's, a stipend of $600 for only three years, and his father's law library if he stuck to the legal profession. 'Dashing and impetuous' and a great orator, he must have antagonized his father. The judgment was too harsh. Ryerson claimed that the last 'severe illness' had affected Sandfield 'both mentally and physically,' making him pretty hard to live with.[7] Henry never uttered publicly an 'unkind word' or 'ceased to honour his father's memory.' He became a brilliant lawyer and editor of the *Freeholder*, split with MacLennan and set up a rival firm, and seemed headed for politics when he died suddenly in 1887. By then he had left the Catholic faith.

In 1874 Adele married Colonel George Pemberton and with Louise resided in England. Josephine, who became the great matriarch of the extended family, survived until 1930. 'Georgie' lived until 1939 and perhaps his life reflected in some way the strange problem of his father's character. He went to the University of Toronto where he starred in academic work and rowing; he helped organize and became first editor of the *Varsity* and fought strenuously for co-education and other women's rights. In 1888 he was called to the bar and nominally headed his late brother's firm. He finally settled in Florida after his mother's death. Meanwhile he had developed rather peculiar personal habits. When he died, he was buried by request 'without benefit of coffin or clergy,' 'wrapped in a blanket held in place by safety pins, then laid on a wide plank of proper length.'[8]

The three great tormentors of Sandfield's life, Brown, Hincks, and Scott, all survived him. Only Brown, his greatest foe and, by reaction, perhaps the most important influence on his political career, seemed moved by his passing. A few years later, Senator Brown was enjoying a party attended by Josephine Langlois at the residence of Prime Minister Alexander Mackenzie. Brown and Sandfield's daughter had

7 Sissons, *My Dearest Sophie*, p. 223, Ryerson to Sophie, 2 June 1872.
8 Langlois Papers, C. B. Waller to Eugene J. Langlois, 27 June 1939.

a joyous exchange reviewing the 'old times when she and her sisters were girls – and could hardly get decent socks from their papa – and I protested against it to him – to his intense delight.'[9]

Enigmatic and just short of greatness, that was the Baldwinite of Cornwall. He had given his province four good years of service as chief minister. But his country was not Ontario; it was Canada. Perhaps psychologically it was the old provincial Canada, geographically centred in the upper St Lawrence and Ottawa valleys, rather than the new dominion of Canada. Yet his mind encompassed the Maritimes and dimly the west; certainly it encompassed the north with all its problems and permanent challenges.

But the Grits could not be put off. Since the mid-fifties they and their Torontonian chief had seen Upper Canada as rightfully theirs, to be saved from the barbarians, the 'Corruptionists' and the 'Coalitionists.' They now had Ontario, and they would keep it until 1905. When it fell from their grip, both they and their province had changed. The man who finally administered the defeat was John Pliny Whitney, who had studied law in the boisterous office of John Sandfield Macdonald. Whitney, who came from a Reform background, claimed that John Sandfield had been not only his legal but also his political tutor. 'My political views and ideas,' he claimed, 'are largely formed upon his.'[10] Whitney was a Conservative but claimed to be a Baldwinite Conservative not a Toronto Tory. Aided by T. C. Patteson, who died before its completion, Whitney saw to the erection in 1909 of a large statue of his mentor before the legislative building in Queen's Park. At the unveiling,[11] he called John Sandfield Macdonald a conscientious and stubborn man of 'great force of character and individuality,' unable often to fit into the normal party moulds or to be a 'successful' political manager. 'No single act of wrong-doing in office to serve his own personal ends can be charged against him.' In this even the *Globe* concurred: 'by no means unprogressive,' Sandfield was 'perfectly trustworthy in the management of the public finances.' Premier Whitney wrote to Josephine shortly after the unveiling of the statue. Its erection had been

9 Brown Papers, Brown to Anne Brown, 18 Feb. 1878.
10 PAO, Whitney Papers, J. P. Whitney to W. Gibbens, 25 April 1907.
11 *Proceedings at the Unveiling of the Statue of John Sandfield Macdonald, First Prime Minister of Ontario, in the Queen's Park, Toronto, November 16th, 1909* (Toronto 1909).

a 'very great satisfaction,' he claimed, partly because in 'my public life I have acted upon, followed and been guided by the ideas which I have often heard him express, and which more than once he expressed to me personally.'[12] In at least one vital respect, however, Whitney and Sandfield were diverse. By the time the Conservatives had won Ontario, they had accepted the classical, provincial-rights federalism of Brown (after 1866), Blake and Mowat. It was the very federalism against which the two Macdonalds had vainly fought.

Of all the tributes which flowed in that June of 1872, one from Mr Justice W. B. Richards was perhaps closest to the mark. The judge, Stephen's brother, had been the man whom Hincks had favoured over Sandfield for Baldwin's position back in 1851; he was now three years from being appointed first chief justice of Canada. He wrote to Christine as a man with 'a close and undeviating friendship with your husband for more than a quarter of a century with uniform and continuous acts of kindness and regard on his part toward me and mine.' 'I have the means of knowing,' Richards continued, 'that he was often misunderstood and that his actions were frequently wilfully misrepresented.' To a man who was so unselfish, the country owed a great debt of gratitude and after the 'prejudices and passions of the day' had passed away, this would be recognized. The province should be grateful for the fact, Richards concluded, that its first premier administered Ontario so efficiently and accomplished so many reforms.[13]

12 JSM Papers, 15 Feb. 1910.
13 *Ibid.*, 17 June 1872.

A Bibliographical Note

A study of John Sandfield Macdonald presents many problems for the student of history. Three in particular deserve comment. First, the John Sandfield Macdonald–Langlois Papers in the Public Archives of Canada are far from complete and far from voluminous, particularly for the period after 1856. The bulk of them consist of letters to Sandfield from people in his home area, often assistants in his office. He did not keep letter books, although the collection does contain drafts or copies of several of his most important letters. Still, one must search for most of his letters among the surviving collections of those with whom he corresponded; more importantly, one must study the letters of his contemporaries in which he was discussed. Secondly, few issues of the Cornwall *Freeholder* survive; fires in the office of the *Standard-Freeholder,* before the days of microfilm, destroyed the principal files. Because Sandfield owned this little weekly, which normally expressed his views, this deficiency leaves the picture especially incomplete. Fortunately several isolated issues were found scattered among numerous collections in various cities. Thirdly, most of the papers of Josiah Blackburn, Sandfield's journalistic confidant, have been lost for over fifteen years.

Among the other personal papers whose examination is essential for a study of Sandfield Macdonald, certain collections should be mentioned particularly: those of Robert Baldwin (Metropolitan Toronto Central Library), George Brown (Public Archives of Canada/PAC), John A. Macdonald (PAC), and Alexander Mackenzie

(Queen's University). Also useful are the papers of Charles Clarke (Ontario, Dept. of Public Records and Archives), William McDougall (PAC), the McGillivrays (PAC), William Lyon Mackenzie and Charles Lindsay (PAO), the Duke of Newcastle (PAC microfilm), R. W. Scott (PAC), John Stevenson (PAC microfilm), and the Waggamans (Mrs. Quita Brodhead, Wayne, Pa.).

The study could not have been undertaken without wide use of many contemporary newspapers, especially the *Globe* and *Leader* of Toronto, the *London Free Press*, and from 1862 to 1864 the *Quebec Mercury*. The *Journals of the Legislative Assembly* for both the province of Ontario and the province of Canada are invaluable.

One is always indebted to others who have written or collected material on the period. Many books are indispensable, especially J. M. S. Careless, *Brown of the 'Globe'*, 2 vols. (Toronto 1959, 1963); Paul Cornell, *The Alignment of Political Groups in Canada, 1841–1867* (Toronto 1962); J. G. Harkness, *Stormont, Dundas and Glengarry: A History, 1784–1945* (Oshawa 1946); W. L. Morton, *The Critical Years: The Union of British North America, 1857–1873* (Toronto 1964); C. B. Sissons, *Egerton Ryerson: His Life and Letters*, 2 vols. (Toronto 1947) and *My Dearest Sophie: Letters of Egerton Ryerson to his Daughter* (Toronto 1955); Richard B. Splane, *Social Welfare in Ontario: 1791–1893* (Toronto 1965); Peter Waite, *Life and Times of Confederation 1864–1867* (Toronto 1962); Franklin A. Walker, *Catholic Education and Politics in Upper Canada* (Toronto 1955).

Many unpublished theses deal secondarily with Sandfield Macdonald. Two should be mentioned here: Elwood H. Jones, 'Political Aspects of the London *Free Press*: 1858–1867' (Master's thesis, University of Western Ontario, 1964) and Margaret Helen Small, 'A Study of the Dominion and the Provincial Election of 1867 in Ontario' (Master's thesis, Queen's University, 1968).

The author's doctoral dissertation, 'The Political Career of John Sandfield Macdonald to the Fall of his Administration in March, 1864: A Study in Canadian Politics' (Duke University, 1964) deals with a portion of his political life in considerably more detail and with considerably more documentation than was possible in this volume. A paper, 'John Sandfield Macdonald and the Crisis of 1863,' Canadian Historical Association, *Report, 1965*, pp. 30–45, has a particular focus on the most critical point in his pre-Confederation experiences.

Index

Albert Edward, Prince of Wales (Edward VII), 48
Allan, Sir Hugh, 119
Allen, Dr. W. C., 114
Armault, Christina (de Brounner), 10
Arthur, HRH Prince (Duke of Connaught), 107, 108

Bagot, Sir Charles, 14, 15
Baldwin, Robert, 24, 30, 34, 91, 123; leader of Upper Canadian Reformers, 13–21; source of political inspiration, 39, 44–47, 69, 76, 85, 92, 96, 105, 111–12
Bell, Robert, 85
Bernard, Hewitt, 87
Bethune, Angus, 114
Bethune, James, 114, 117
Blackburn, Josiah (editor, London *Free Press*), 42–48, 50–58, 62, 65, 76, 92
Blackburn, Stephen, 65
Blake, Edward, 91–97, 103, 104, 111–17, 119, 123
Blake, William Hume, 18, 91
Brock, General Sir Isaac, 6
Brounner, Baron de, 10
Brounner, Maria de (Carbonara), Baroness de Brounner, 10
Brown, Anne (Nelson), Mrs. George Brown, 64, 76, 83, 91, 93
Brown, George (editor, Toronto *Globe*), 3, 24, 51–53, 55, 120, 123; works closely with JSM, 18–22, 27–31; developing split with JSM 33–49; attitude to JSM's government, 57, 60, 62, 66–68, 70–72; opposes the Scott Bill (1863), 63–65; Confederation, 75, 77–82, 84; on JSM's family, 76–77, 121–22; opposes the Patent Combination, 85–94, 97–99, 101–06, 111–14
Brown, Gordon, 63
Brydges, C. J., 58, 103, 119
Buchanan, Isaac, 9
Bujac, Mlle, 10

Cameron, John Hillyard, 81
Cameron, Malcolm, 65
Cameron, Matthew Crooks: opposes Confederation, 81; Ontario cabinet minister, 88, 91, 94, 96, 97, 107, 112, 114; becomes leader of the opposition, 117

Carling, John, 50, 88, 109, 111, 113, 117
Cartier, George Etienne, 30, 53, 67, 73, 101, 104, 108; Bleu leader, 35, 37; premier, 38, 40, 45, 50, 51; his militia bill, 54, 55, 66; coalition and Confederation, 74–78; intrigues with Reformers, 102–3
Cartwright, Richard, 102
Cauchon, Joseph, 66, 67, 78
Charbonnel, Armand François Marie de (Bishop of Toronto), 20
Charles I, of England, 28
Clarke, Charles, 40, 43
Cockburn, A. P., 109
Colquhoun, William, 90, 114
Connor, Dr. Skeffington, 64
Craig, James, 90, 114
Crooks, Adam, 91

Dorion, Antoine Aimé: Rouge leader, 29, 35, 37–39, 42, 45, 48–52, 55, 66; in JSM's cabinet, 56, 60, 67–69, 74; opposes Confederation, 75, 77, 84; steadfast liberal, 85, 87, 95
Draper, William Henry, 9–15, 16, 40–43, 107
Dix, General John A., 72
Doyle, J. E., 46, 49
Drummond, L. T., 38, 67
Dufresne, Alexandre, 78
Durham, John George Lambton, 1st Earl of, 11, 17

Elgin, James Bruce, 8th Earl of, 16, 18, 23, 27, 28, 30, 59

Ferguson, T. R., 49
Fleming, Sir Sanford, 69, 72
Foley, Michael: moderate Reformer, 31, 38, 45, 46, 48, 49, 51, 53, 55; in JSM's cabinet, 57, 62, 67; opposes JSM, 68, 72, 91
Forbes, Horace, 104, 105
Fraser, Colonel Alexander, 11–19, 27
Fraser, Archibald, 36
Freeholder (Cornwall), 16, 18, 43, 46, 49, 51, 52, 83, 84, 102, 121
Free Press (London) (*see* Blackburn, Josiah, for editorial references)

Galt, Sir Alexander Tilloch, 37, 38, 41, 50, 71, 84–86, 102–4
George III, of England, 6
Gibbs, Thomas Nicholson, 91
Gladstone, William Ewart, 60, 61
Globe (Toronto) (*see* Brown, George, for editorial references)
Gordon, Sir Arthur, 71
Grant, Dr. James, 12, 15, 21
Grant, General Ulysses S., 108
Grey, Henry George Grey, 3rd Earl, 16

Hamel, Théophile, 28
Haultain, Colonel Frederick William, 78
Head, Sir Edmund Walker, 38, 40, 59
Hincks, Sir Francis, 14, 17, 18, 20–31, 101–4, 111, 121, 123
Hodgins, J. G., 97
Holton, Luther Hamilton: Lower Canadian Liberal friend of George Brown, 37, 38, 42, 45, 48, 51, 60; in JSM's cabinet, 67–69, 71–73; on Confederation 75–77; opposes continued coalition (1866–67) 85–87
Horan, Bishop E. J., 65
Howe, Joseph, 59, 92, 93, 101
Howland, William P.: in JSM's cabinet, 57, 63, 66, 67; mission to London, 60, 61; remains in Coalition (1866–67) 84, 86, 87; lieutenant governor of Ontario, 100, 115

Ivy Hall (Sandfield Macdonald family home), 19, 22, 27, 32, 35, 46, 56, 62, 76, 83, 95, 107, 108, 118–20

Jackson, General Andrew, 10
James I, of England, 28
Jervois, Colonel W. F. O., 72

King, E. H., 103, 119

Laberge, C. J., 34
Lafontaine, Sir Louis Hippolyte, 14, 15, 17, 19–21, 34, 45, 69
Langlois, Eugene, 110
Langlois, Jean, 108
Langlois, Josephine (*see* Macdonald, Mary-Josephine)
Langmuir, J. W., 98, 111
Langton, John, 73
Laurier, Sir Wilfrid, 60
Lee, General Robert E., 62
Lincoln, Abraham, 52, 72
Lynch, Bishop John Joseph, 65

Macdonald, Adele (Sandfield), Mrs. George Pemberton, 27, 121
Macdonald, Agnes (Bernard), Lady Macdonald, 101, 110
Macdonald, Alexander Francis (Sandfield), 7, 32, 119, 120
Macdonald, Alexander Sandfield, 7
Macdonald, Allan, 7
Macdonald, Catherine (Fraser), Mrs. Donald Alexander (Sandfield) Macdonald, 26
Macdonald, Cecilla Cora (Sandfield), 46, 49
Macdonald, Donald Alexander (Sandfield), 7, 119; early career, 15, 25–27; opposes separate schools in Glengarry, 24, 31–34, 46, 53; Reform member for Glengarry, 36, 37, 44, 48, 49, 51, 53, 64, 67; opposes Confederation, 81; against Fenians 84; ambivalent politics (1867–71), 86, 90, 103, 114, 116, 117
Macdonald, George Sandfield, 46, 121
Macdonald, Henry Sandfield, 19, 83, 121
Macdonald, John (of Knoydart), 7
Macdonald, Sir John Alexander: Upper Canadian Conservative leader (to 1863), 27, 28, 30, 34–37, 44, 45, 48–51, 55, 64; opposes Sandfield Macdonald's government, 65–68, 72, 74; on Confederation, 75–80, 82, 84–85; role in securing Ontario premiership for JSM, 3, 86–89; election of 1867, 88–92; relations with JSM as premier (1867–71), 94–96, 99–106, 108, 110–14, 116, 117, 123
Macdonald, Lilla Sandfield, 15, 47, 76, 121, 122
Macdonald, Louise Christine (Sandfield), Mrs. J. G. Uppleby 16, 76, 106–8, 121, 122
Macdonald, Marie Christine (Waggaman), Mrs. John Sandfield Macdonald: courtship 5,10; married life (to 1862), 11, 13–16, 19, 23, 27, 46; wife of Canadian premier, 56, 71, 73, 76, 77; and Southern relatives during Civil War, 52, 62; after the War, 83–84; wife of Ontario premier, 106, 108–10; death of husband, 119, 123; later life, 121
Macdonald, Mary Josephine (Sandfield), Mrs. Jean Langlois, 16, 76, 77, 107, 108, 110, 121, 122
Macdonald, Nancy, Mrs. Alexander Sandfield Macdonald, 7
Macdonald, Ranald Sandfield, 7, 25, 26, 32
Macdonell, Bishop Alexander, 8

Macdonell, Rev. Alexander (Scotus), 6, 7
Macdonell, Colonel John (Greenfield), 6, 7
Macdonell, Colonel John (Leek), 6, 7, 12
McDougall, William: Clear Grit radical, 20, 26, 27, 31; Brownite, 44, 49, 53; in JSM's cabinet, 57, 63, 64, 72; on Confederation 75; remains in coalition (1866–69), 84, 86, 87, 90, 91, 93, 101; in the Northwest, 101, 102
McGee, Thomas D'Arcy: Montreal Irish Liberal, 38, 40, 48, 53; in Sandfield Macdonald's cabinet, 56, 59, 60, 65–67; opposes Sandfield Macdonald, 68, 72, 111; on Confederation, 75
McGillivray, John, 11–14
McIntyre, Dr. Daniel E., 19, 21, 24–26, 30
McKellar, Archibald, 91, 94, 112, 116
Mackenzie, Alexander, 57, 66, 82, 91, 103, 114–16, 121
MacKenzie, Alexander M., 19, 20, 24, 25, 32, 33, 90
McKenzie, Rev. John, 12
Mackenzie, William Lyon, 21, 22, 30, 35, 99
McLachlan, Rev. (Spanish) John, 31, 32
McLean, Alexander, 12, 13, 16, 17
McLean, Archibald, 8, 9, 11–13, 32, 46
MacLennan, Donald Ban, 120, 121
MacMahan, Hugh, 111
McMartin, Alexander, 17
MacNab, Sir Allan Napier, 9, 30, 34
Macpherson, Senator David Lewis, 87, 91, 103
Marshall, Charles, 109
Metcalfe, Sir Charles Theophilus, 15, 38
Mills, David, 111
Mitchell, Peter, 84
Monck, Charles Stanley, Viscount, 55, 56, 58–61, 67, 69, 70, 74, 76, 106
Morin, Augustin Norbert, 14, 21, 22, 27, 29, 30
Mowat, Sir Oliver, 38, 49, 50, 53, 57, 66–69, 75, 123

Nelles, Samuel Sobieske, 96
Newcastle, Henry Pelham-Clinton, 5th Duke of, 48, 58–61, 70

Oliver, William, 49, 52

Papineau, Louis Joseph, 18, 22, 28
Patrick, William, 86
Patteson, Thomas Charles, 118, 122
Pemberton, Adele (*see* Macdonald, Adele)
Pemberton, Colonel George, 121
Phelan, Bishop Michael, 17, 24, 30, 32
Pius IX, 20

Quebec Mercury, 57, 58, 62, 64, 65, 68, 69

Richards, Albert N., 72, 90, 91
Richards, Stephen, 88, 91, 94, 107, 109, 114, 123
Richards, W. B., 21, 24, 26, 123
Riel, Louis, 102, 112
Ross, John, 25, 26, 30
Ryerson, Rev. Egerton, 15, 20, 24; on Scott bill crisis (1863), 63–66; friendship with JSM, 66, 76, 83, 92, 108, 121; opposes party government, 92–93; educational reforms, 83, 95–97
Ryerson, Sophie, 76, 77, 108

Scoble, John, 75
Scott, Richard W.: on separate

schools, 53, 58, 63–66, 74; political power in Ottawa valley, 68, 90, 104; role in fall of JSM's government (1871), 104, 115–17, 121
Scott, Thomas, 112
Seward, William Henry, 52, 62, 72
Sheppard, George, 43, 44, 58, 99
Sicotte, Louis Victor: as a Rouge in crisis of 1854, 27–30; co-operation as a Mauve with JSM, 40, 43, 45, 49–53; opposes militia bill (1862), 54–55; associate leader in JSM cabinet, 56, 60, 61, 66, 67; opposes JSM, 68, 70; appointed to the bench, 70
Smith, Frank, 91
Smith, Sir Henry, 94
Smith, Sydney, 76
Snodgrass, Rev. William, 96
Stephen, George, 119
Stisted, Major General William Henry, 87, 93, 94, 109
Strachan, Rev. John, 8
Sumner, Charles, 62
Sydenham, Charles Poulett Thomson, Baron, 12–14

Taché, Bishop Alexandre Antonin
Taché, Sir Etienne Paschal, 33, 34, 63, 73–75
Talbot, Colonel Thomas, 9
Thibaudeau, J.-E., 37, 38, 41, 46, 49
Tilley, Sir Leonard, 59, 61, 69, 71, 78, 79, 84
Todd, Alpheus, 29
Tupper, Sir Charles, 70, 84

Uppleby, J. George, 108
Uppleby, Louise (*see* Macdonald, Louise)
Urquhart, Rev. Hugh, 8

Vankoughnet, Philip, 36
Victoria, Queen, 55, 107, 109

Waggaman, Camille (Armault), Mrs. George Waggaman, 10, 11, 13, 35
Waggaman, Christine (*see* Macdonald, Marie Christine)
Waggaman, Colonel Eugene, 16, 52, 62, 84, 110
Waggaman, George Augustus, 5, 10, 11, 13
Waggaman, Matilda, 10, 16
Wales, Prince of (later Edward VII), 48
Walker, John, 19, 25, 33
Wallbridge, Thomas Campbell, 86
Wallis, Teakle, 10, 11
Watkin, Edward W., 58, 59, 70
Webster, Daniel, 10
Whitney, John Pliny, 122, 123
Wiseman, Nicholas, Cardinal, Archbishop of Westminster, 20
Wood, Edmund Burke, 88, 94, 97, 107, 109, 115